Praise for *Choos*

A provocative and practical read! Seda and Brown provide an opportunity for us to examine our own practices and beliefs and engage in transformative discussions with colleagues around equity in the mathematics classroom through the seven principles of the ICUCARE equity framework. Seda and Brown remind us that equity is not a destination but a journey we take together with our students, their families, and our colleagues.

—**Dr. Trena L. Wilkerson,** professor, Department of Curriculum and Instruction, Baylor University, president, NCTM

Too often, equity in mathematics education is positioned primarily as theoretical and heart work. I appreciate how Drs. Seda and Brown present the ICUCARE equity framework as tangible work based on strong theoretical grounding.

—**Robert Q. Berry III, PhD,** Samuel Braley Gray professor of Mathematics Education, associate dean of Diversity, Equity, and Inclusion, University of Virginia's School of Education and Human Development

This book uses an ethic of care to offer teachers a set of principles that can be used to provide all children, especially those from historically excluded backgrounds, with culturally relevant mathematics education. It's one thing to embrace Standards for Mathematics Practices (SMP) but quite another to see the human potential of minoritized children and teach them in ways that ensure they actually succeed. The authors of this book share rich personal stories that not only help teachers to see their students but to also perceive who they are and what they can become.

—**Jacqueline Leonard,** professor of Mathematics Education, University of Wyoming

This book helps close the gap between recognizing that we can do more to make math classrooms equitable and actually having a plan for how to do it. Pamela and Kyndall are respected leaders in the mathematics education community and help unpack the problems we may not be aware of as well as solutions for addressing them.

This is an excellent resource that provides teachers and teacher leaders with timely scholarly literature, opportunities for self-reflection (we must truly see in order to do), and a framework for taking action.

Choosing to See is a wonderful resource for new and veteran teachers alike. With authentic vignettes, explicit strategies, and a wealth of research, the book is an essential addition to the library of any teacher committed to addressing and preventing inequities in the mathematics classroom.

Choosing to See is the emotional and spiritual journey that all math educators need to embark on wholeheartedly. The book is a timely primer that takes the deep and complex issue of race and systemic bias in the mathematical experiences of Black students and presents them with unflinching clarity and candor.

No matter where you are in your own journey to becoming a student of your students, you will find inspiration in stories from the hearts of teachers and find clear, actionable ideas about routes to take and stops to make along the way.

Choosing to See is more than just another book about equity in mathematics. Seda and Brown's ICUCARE framework helps educators understand why something is an equity issue and how to take action to change the narrative.

This timely book provides guidance for mathematics teachers and teacher educators who want to learn how to enact equity in mathematics classrooms. Building on research, stories, and professional expertise, the chapters illustrate how to notice students' strengths, reflect on power dynamics, and enact a caring pedagogy.

—Judit Moschkovich, professor, Mathematics Education, University of California, Santa Cruz

Pamela Seda and Kyndall Brown share personal stories and a compelling call to action to truly see students for who they are, to understand students' cultural backgrounds and identify their strengths, and to erase the effects of negative stereotypes on the educational outcomes of marginalized students.

—Mona Toncheff, president, NCSM

Pamela Seda and Kyndall Brown introduce the ICUCARE framework, which moves beyond talking the talk of equity and social justice and provides a pathway for teachers to walk the walk. This framework also empowers students to exercise their agency as creators and doers of mathematics. Perhaps most important, Seda and Brown confront and disempower deficit framings and stereotypes that have been imposed on many students.

—Danny Bernard Martin, University of Illinois at Chicago

Pamela Seda and Kyndall Brown not only make us conscious of what we don't see, they provide a wonderful and enlightening roadmap—ICUCARE—for overcoming our functional hypocrisy with meaningful and practical actions for our classroom, our teacher teams, our school, and most importantly our students.

—Timothy D. Kanold, PhD

In *Choosing to See,* Pamela Seda and Kyndall Brown return our eyes to the powerful truth that teaching and learning require each of us to engage in genuine human exchanges. The ICUCARE framework empowers teachers to engage the schooling system to act in anti-racist, anti-othering ways.

—Christopher S. Brownell, PhD, associate professor of Math and STEM Education, Fresno Pacific University

Choosing to See offers invaluable ideas and techniques for every facet of your practice—social, pedagogical, mathematical, and more. Seda and Brown will transform the way you see your students inside your classroom and also the world outside your classroom.

—Dan Meyer, chief academic officer, Desmos

As educators, we are continually looking to create a learning space where all students feel valued, but we have to be intentional. If we're seeking to build a classroom culture that is as inclusive and diverse as the students we teach, this is the framework we need.

—Graham Fletcher, Atlanta, GA, math specialist

A supportive guide to far more equitable teaching in which teachers aren't blamed; they are given tools to be more self-reflective. Teachers aren't assumed to be biased; they are taught to be far more socially conscious. And teachers who casually assert that they are color-blind are gently nudged to become color-conscious. I urge all teachers to add this accessible, practical, and informative book to their list of required reading.

—Steve Leinwand, researcher,
American Institutes for Research

This book provides multiple practical resources that can be implemented immediately. By following the tips and strategies in this book, one will improve their instructional practices, increase their students' engagement, and learn to see the brilliance in every student.

—Dr. Kristopher Childs, chief equity and
social justice officer, Open Up Resources

This book provides the tools to help teachers look in the mirror as a part of their instructional regime, not only to see themselves but to provide a scaffold to observe their students in relationship to mathematics learning, the broader community, and culture.

—William F. Tate IV, Education Foundation Distinguished
Professor in Sociology, University of South Carolina-Columbia

Teachers, teacher educators, and leaders can use this book as part of their professional learning communities to position all students for success in mathematics classrooms. For many historically underserved student populations, success in mathematics still remains a dream. This book illuminates how to make that dream a reality.

—**Sylvia Celedón-Pattichis, PhD,** professor, Department of Language, Literacy, and Sociocultural Studies, College of Education and Human Sciences, University of New Mexico

This book is a must-read for math educators. *Choosing to See* offers a helpful framework, sound advice, and plenty of examples to show you a path from good intentions to practical action.

—**Francis Su,** author of *Mathematics for Human Flourishing*

Choosing to See makes a persuasive case for change based on formidable social justice imperatives and data, and communicates a sense of urgency and shared responsibility to replace archaic teaching practices with the suggested high-leverage resources included in this text.

—**Christina Lincoln-Moore,** principal, Cheremoya Avenue Elementary, Los Angeles Unified School District

Choosing to See

CHOOSING
TO SEE

A FRAMEWORK FOR EQUITY
IN THE MATH CLASSROOM

PAMELA SEDA & KYNDALL BROWN

Choosing to See: A Framework for Equity in the Math Classroom
© 2021 Pamela Seda and Kyndall Brown

This book is available at special discounts when purchased in quantity for educational purposes or for use as premiums, promotions, or fundraisers. For inquiries and details, contact the publisher at books@daveburgessconsulting.com.

Published by Dave Burgess Consulting, Inc.
San Diego, CA
DaveBurgessConsulting.com

Library of Congress Control Number: 2021933580
Paperback ISBN: 978-1-951600-80-8
Ebook ISBN: 978-1-951600-81-5

Cover illustration by Candace Seda
Photo of Kyndall Brown by Harmon Outlaw
Photo of Pamela Seda by Brian Jones Photography

Cover and interior design by Liz Schreiter
Editing and production by Reading List Editorial: readinglisteditorial.com

We dedicate this book to our parents, the late TSgt Cornelius & Girlie Jones and General L. & Eleanor Brown. We are the sum total of their love, care, time, energy, and sacrifice.

CONTENTS

CONTENTS

FOREWORD

For the last three decades, I have been sharing the findings from a National Academy of Education/Spencer Postdoctoral Fellowship. In 1989, when I first began my research on teachers who were successful with African American students, it never occurred to me that it would be part of a career-long journey to understand the ways that pedagogy impacts student learning. Spending three years in the classrooms of masterful teachers showed me what a difference teaching can make in the lives of students—particularly those students who have been underserved by traditional schooling.

I have had the pleasure of telling these teachers' stories and crafting their work into a theory with three propositions—focusing on student learning, supporting cultural competence, and developing critical consciousness. This work has taken me around the world—Umeå, Sweden; London, England; Edinburgh, Scotland; Melbourne, Australia; Belo Horizonte, Brazil; Bloemfontein, South Africa; Beijing, China; Tokyo, Japan—and across the United States. Despite this work being warmly received by teachers, administrators, teacher education students, graduate students, and community members, one group of people has remained skeptical of the message of culturally relevant pedagogy: those teaching in STEM (science, technology, engineering, and mathematics) fields. Despite having some of the poorest outcomes for BIPOC (Black, Indigenous, and people of color) students, many in these fields insist that culture does not play a role in their discipline and culturally relevant pedagogy does not apply to them.

This volume, *Choosing to See: A Framework for Equity in the Math Classroom,* is an important corrective to the myth that mathematics is abstract and therefore not influenced by culture. Something as simple as how we count has a cultural component. Many years ago, while participating in a workshop at the National Academy of Science while working on the first iteration of the report, *How People Learn: Brain, Mind, Experience and School,* we heard from a colleague who studied how young Chinese students learned mathematics, specifically counting. One of the eye-opening statements was that the Mandarin language has no equivalent to the words *eleven* and *twelve.* In their language, *eleven* is actually said as "ten plus one" and *twelve* as "ten plus two." Interesting, mathematics as it is taught in US schools is dependent on a base ten, but we have this odd eleven and twelve linguistic construction. This is not just "mathematics." It is mathematics in a cultural context.

In my study, I was struck by the sixth-grade teacher who decided to forgo the district-mandated curriculum and scrounged for algebra I books so she could accelerate the teaching and learning for a class of African American students who would likely be discouraged from pursuing algebra when they got to eighth grade. The teacher decided to embed the teaching of algebra in deeply cultural contexts and demonstrated most of the principles highlighted in this volume: including others as experts; being critically conscious; understanding her students; crafting a culturally relevant curriculum; assessing, activating, and building on students' prior knowledge; releasing and sharing control with students (and families); and demanding and expecting more.

Later in this journey, I heard from mathematics educator Dr. Lee Stiff about how he designed an algebra I course for students struggling in "general math." Again, Stiff used the principles that are outlined in this volume. His attitude toward the work was, "Nothing we do can hurt these kids," because the quality of the general mathematics curriculum was so poor that mastering one or two algebra I concepts was more valuable than a year's worth of addition, subtraction, multiplication, and division of whole numbers and fractions.

This volume asks mathematics teachers to teach ambitious mathematics in cultural contexts that students understand and appreciate. It does not ask teachers to compromise the mathematics, but it also does not ask teachers to prioritize the mathematics above the students' interests and well-being. This work goes beyond Carol Dweck's notion of a growth mindset or Angela Duckworth's concept of grit. Instead, *Choosing to See* places responsibility on teachers to learn much more about students as they approach teaching mathematics. Instead of assuming that mathematics is culture-neutral, teachers must begin to interrogate how the mathematics curriculum fails to take into account students' backgrounds, cultural contexts, and experiences.

Dr. Jamaal Sharif Matthews of the University of Michigan conducted a National Science Foundation–sponsored project to look at the relationship between teachers' math applications to students' everyday experience and adolescent cognitive flexibility. This work indicates that when students can see how mathematics applies to the world they recognize and understand, they perform better in mathematics. Again, Dr. Matthews demonstrates that the principles being espoused here in *Choosing to See* are important for ensuring all students experience mathematics success.

It is exciting to see mathematics educators move away from notions that "only certain students" will be proficient in mathematics to Robert Moses's idea of mathematics as a civil right. The world our students are entering is increasingly complex and mathematized. Students require more than a rudimentary knowledge of mathematics to have economic and social success in a highly technological, globally interconnected world. The demands of a complex democracy require students who can make sense of a scientific and technology-laden world. *Choosing to See: A Framework for Equity in the Math Classroom* is the volume today's teachers will need to help students navigate that world.

Gloria Ladson-Billings
University of Wisconsin–Madison
September 2020

WHY WE'VE WRITTEN THIS BOOK

—————— **Pam's Story** ——————

Growing up, being Black was just a part of who I was, like being a girl or having brown eyes. I never really thought about my race being a liability, but it never really gave me a sense of pride, either. I was pretty neutral about it. However, that changed when I got to college. Even though Georgia Tech was where I was called the "N word" by a White person for the first time in my life, it was also the place where I first felt such a sense of pride in being African American and the need to advocate for the success of African American students collectively in an institution where there were so few of us. I felt this pride when we elected our first Black homecoming queen and had our first Black cheerleader. That pride continued as we strategized how we would elect a record number of Black students to student council positions. I understood and experienced Black excellence and the power of working together to make a difference in our school, and I felt that same sense of pride in our collective efficacy.

During my first years of teaching, I taught math in a high school that was pretty evenly divided between Black and White students. However, the teaching staff was predominantly White. I recall times when African American students whom I had never taught would try to connect with me on a personal level by approaching me in the cafeteria or the hall just to say hi, to compliment me on my outfit, or to congratulate me on my pregnancy. I don't remember this ever happening with White students at the school. It was then that I began to realize I was a role model for many of the Black students and that my presence gave them a sense of who they could be. I also began to understand that my presence as a young African American woman in that school challenged the negative stereotypes about who is good at math.

I am an African American woman who is passionate about changing the negative experiences of students who have not previously experienced mathematical success. "Success," to me, is not simply passing a class, but rather being able to use mathematics as a tool to reason, analyze, communicate, and open doors of opportunity. Too often, mathematics has been taught in a manner where students cease to think on their own, instead memorizing meaningless routines and procedures just to get by. Rather than mathematics leading to opportunity, mathematical failure often results in lack of self-esteem, frustration, heartache, and shattered dreams for furthering education. For me, the mathematics classroom was a place where I took great delight in making connections, reasoning, and analyzing mathematical ideas in an environment where I was valued, esteemed, and confident. In other words, I not only felt "smart" in class, I was constantly told as much by my teachers, classmates, and friends. It did not take me very long, however, to realize that many people did not share this experience and that, for them, mathematics class meant confusion, failure, self-doubt, and feeling like a "dummy."

I became a teacher because I wanted my students to experience mathematics the way I did—as something positive and empowering. I have written this book because I want more teachers to have positive and empowering mathematics classrooms for their students from marginalized groups.[1]

Kyndall's Story

I am a descendant of Africans who were enslaved in America. My parents were born into segregated Alabama in the 1930s. They grew up in incredibly supportive and nurturing communities, surrounded by families that encouraged them to get their education and continue to advance the race. Both of my parents attended historically Black colleges and universities. My father studied education at Alabama State University (his diploma says "Alabama State College for Negroes"), and my mother pursued a career in dental hygiene at Howard University. My parents met, married, and started a family. I was born in the early 1960s, at the height of the civil rights movement. Seeking economic security, my parents left Alabama for what Isabel Wilkerson calls "the warmth of other suns."

They settled in Los Angeles, California, where my father got a job as an English teacher, and my mother was able to practice her craft as a dental hygienist. In 1967, we moved into the View Park–Windsor Hills neighborhood, which would become one of the wealthiest Black neighborhoods in the United States. I grew up in an environment of single-family homes with two-parent families, where the majority of adults were college-educated professionals, civil service employees, and small- and large-business owners.

The elementary school in our community was high achieving and predominantly Black. When I was in the third grade, our school received the highest scores in reading on the district standardized test. This achievement led to features about our school in the local

1   Pamela Seda, "Equity Pedagogy in the Secondary Mathematics Classrooms of Three Preservice Teachers" (PhD dissertation, Georgia State University, 2008), 66.

newspaper and on the local television stations. Going to school in this environment solidified my belief that academic success was compatible with my identity as a person of African descent.

After elementary school, most of the children in my neighborhood participated in a voluntary busing program to junior high schools in predominantly White neighborhoods. While we were bused into the schools for the purposes of integration, many of the academic classes were segregated. Because I was on a college preparatory track, I was often one of the few Black students in my English, mathematics, science, and social studies classes. The only classes I had with most of my Black peers were electives and physical education.

The curriculum at my school was very Eurocentric. Through my entire time in junior high, I never had a Black teacher. Still, I did have some teachers who were engaging, like my algebra teacher, Mr. Perlman. He was a pretty traditional teacher by today's standards. He wrote notes on the board, and we copied them into our notebooks. But there was something about the way he taught the properties of equality and how to use them to solve equations that stuck, and it was in junior high school that I fell in love with algebra.

My high school experience was similar to junior high. I was bused to a predominantly White high school. By taking a college preparatory course load, I was again often one of few Black students in class. One noteworthy difference, though, was that I had my first Black mathematics teacher: Mrs. Garner. She taught algebra II, and we lived in the same neighborhood. She recognized my potential and nurtured me. This contrasted sharply with an experience I had my senior year in my trigonometry and math analysis class, where I had a White female teacher who put Bs and Ws in her roll book to identify the race of her students.

I ended up attending college at the University of California, Irvine, where I majored in mathematics. Once again, I was one of the few Black students in most of my classes, and I survived by finding groups to study and do homework with. After graduation, I began my teaching career in South Los Angeles during the height of the gang and drug crisis. I found that, although many of my students came from impoverished backgrounds, they had a lot of problem-solving skills.

In those early days, I realized that even though I had a degree in mathematics, I still had a lot to learn about how to be an effective teacher. I sought out professional learning opportunities wherever I could and enrolled in a teacher credentialing program, and I have continued throughout my career to pursue educational opportunities to improve my craft. Along the way, I have gotten involved with teacher education and professional development, and because of my background and experiences, I have always been committed to ensuring Black students have opportunities to receive high-quality mathematics instruction and access to college preparatory mathematics classes. My hope for this book is that it will be a tool for teachers of students of color in general, and students of African descent in particular, that will help them recognize their students' potential to be powerful mathematical thinkers.

INTRODUCTION

WHAT IS AT STAKE

Mathematics has the power to shatter students' dreams in a number of ways. Students are assessed in mathematics in some states as early as kindergarten. Standardized test scores are used to label and sort students in ways that impact the types of learning experiences they receive (whether they receive remediation versus enrichment, for example). These labels often follow children into higher grades, limiting their access to high-quality mathematics instruction.

In high school, mathematics plays a role in whether students meet their graduation requirements, with most schools stipulating two to four years of math classes. The mathematics courses schools offer determine whether or not students will meet college entrance requirements.

Similarly, at the college level, a large number of students test into remedial mathematics courses where they get stuck and are never able to realize their goal of obtaining a college degree. Most of the top jobs for the future require students to have a strong foundational understanding of mathematics (e.g., solar energy technician, software developer, data analyst). Our failure to mathematically educate most students in general, and students of color in particular, is bad not only for these students individually, but also for our society.

If schools at all levels are not prepared to support students who arrive with gaps in their mathematical knowledge, then students enter into a cycle of failing and repeating classes until, eventually, they give up and drop out. Though most school mission statements have some variation of "all" or "every" or "each" student, math data for the past thirty years have clearly shown that we are missing the mark for so many. If we truly value "all" of our students, we must figure out how to make sure our actions align with our values. An equity framework can serve as a lens for helping us see where we are achieving this alignment and where we are not.

ICUCARE EQUITY FRAMEWORK

One day, after Pam had finished leading a workshop on the equity framework she created, one of the participants said, "This is really great stuff, but you need to come up with a mnemonic device to help us remember the principles." That conversation sparked the ICUCARE (pronounced "I See You Care") framework we will explore in this book.

There are seven principles in our equity framework:

- Include others as experts
- Be Critically conscious
- Understand your students
- Use Culturally relevant curricula
- Assess, activate, and build on prior knowledge
- Release control
- Expect more

ICUCARE is about choosing to see and caring enough about what you see to act. It means accepting that every one of your students can be an expert given the opportunity. It means recognizing negative stereotypes about marginalized students and understanding their effects. It means knowing that your students have rich lives outside of the classroom that can inform what you do inside the classroom. It means embracing that doers of mathematics come in all ethnicities, genders, and races. It means appreciating the wealth of knowledge that students bring with them to any given topic. It means viewing your students as co-laborers in the process of teaching and learning. And it means valuing students in terms of their strengths, capabilities, and talents.

There are many reasons teachers choose not to truly see their students in all of their humanity and to ignore how prevalent inequity is in our educational system. Like we did early in our teaching careers, many teachers find it easier not to see than to acknowledge their own failures as educators. It was easier for us to see students' lack of motivation, their failure to turn in assignments, their refusal to follow instructions, and their lack of parental support. For Pam, it wasn't until she saw data that showed the Black males in her remedial math classes scored significantly higher on the national normed test than the White students in the same class that she started to see the school structures—including her own—that were also operating on students. And once she began to "see," she sought to find answers in a doctoral program focused on issues of race, class, and gender in mathematics education. True "seeing" must always precede doing.

Although ICUCARE places these principles in order, no order of implementation is indicated by their listing in this manner. It is important to note, there is plenty of overlap between principles, with many examples and strategies aligning to more than one principle. For example, the instructional strategy Two Minute Talks involves pairs of students taking turns telling everything they know about the topic of the day in one minute. This strategy addresses the principle of *Assess, Activate, and Build on Prior Knowledge* because it reminds students of things they may have forgotten about the topic, and it builds background knowledge for students who didn't previously have it. When students say, "I had forgotten …," their knowledge is being activated. When they say, "I didn't know …," their background knowledge is being built. Two Minute Talks address *Release Control* because students get to direct their conversations about the topic by choosing what they want to share, rather than the teacher choosing for them. It addresses *Include Others as Experts* because students are learning from the expertise of their classmates. Every student knows something about a topic, and they each have the opportunity to share that information with others. It also addresses *Expect More* because it begins with the premise that all students have some prior knowledge, and it doesn't allow low-achieving students to opt out. Because every student must talk for at least one minute, no one is let off the hook for engaging with the topic.

Color-blindness and inequitable teaching practices

These principles also overlap in other ways. Teachers who ascribe to a color-blind ideology are not critically conscious. In addition, their ability to understand their students well is hindered because they choose to see their students only as individuals and not as part of a larger cultural group. Therefore, they are cut off from a wealth of cultural knowledge about their students that could be used to communicate mathematical concepts and provide the scaffolding necessary for learning. When teachers fail to build on prior knowledge, their students often begin to experience academic failure. Faced with poor performance from their diverse learners, these teachers then begin to develop deficit views of them.

Teachers with cultural backgrounds different from their students' who fail to ascertain and value the knowledge and skills their students bring with them must resort to making assumptions, which are often based on stereotypes and misinformation.[1] Therefore, when their students perform poorly, teachers tend to blame the individual, citing such issues as laziness, low motivation, or lack of support at

---

1   Beverly Tatum, *Why Are All the Black Kids Sitting Together in the Cafeteria? And Other Conversations about Race* (New York: Basic Books, 1997).

home, rather than implicate their own lack of pedagogical knowledge. The following diagram illustrates how these principles overlap and impact each other.

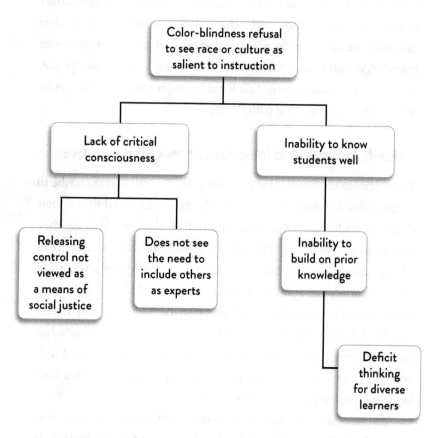

Relationship of color-blindness to equity pedagogy

Communicating this framework to students

It is important that teachers who desire to implement these principles in their classrooms share this framework with their students. Students and teachers often have competing agendas in mathematics classrooms. Without clear communication, a teacher seeking to *Include Others as Experts* may be perceived by her students as not wanting to give them help. A teacher who decides to *Expect More* of her students may be perceived as picking on them or trying to embarrass them. Without the cooperation of students, a "warm demander" may just come across as demanding without the warmth. For this reason, we recommend engaging your students as partners in implementing this framework by creating a student version that mirrors the original in ways students will understand.

- Include others as experts—Look beyond the expertise of the teacher to recognize your own competence and that of your classmates.
- Be Critically conscious—Understand how negative stereotypes impact the educational outcomes of students of color and actively work to erase the effects of those negative stereotypes in yourself, your classroom, your school, and your community.
- Understand how relationships improve learning—Get to know your teacher and classmates in ways that support the socio-emotional aspect of learning.
- Use Culturally relevant resources—Seek out resources that help you see yourself as a doer of mathematics and help you overcome the negative stereotypes and messages about who is mathematically smart.
- Assess, activate, and build on prior knowledge—Value the prior knowledge that you bring to the classroom (no one comes as a blank slate) and build on that prior knowledge to help you learn new things.

- **R**etain control—Take ownership of your own learning by focusing on sensemaking and not allowing others to GPS you. (Giving step-by-step directions that make no sense, rather than giving help in ways that allows students to understand the process. This concept is discussed further in the "Be a warm demander" section of chapter 7.)
- **E**xpect more—Expect more from yourself and your classmates by rising above the low expectations that others may set for you.

These were written in such a way that students were not only informed but also empowered to become participants in their own liberation from the effects of negative stereotypes. Although the version above was written for high school students, the language can be adapted to engage students at any level.

EQUITY AND THE STANDARDS FOR MATHEMATICAL PRACTICE

The Standards for Mathematical Practice (SMP) provide a template for high-quality mathematics instruction. These standards are as follows:

1. Make sense of problems and persevere in solving them.
2. Reason abstractly and quantitatively.
3. Construct viable arguments and critique the reasoning of others.
4. Model with mathematics.
5. Use appropriate tools strategically.
6. Attend to precision.
7. Look for and make use of structure.
8. Look for and express regularity in repeated reasoning.

The Common Core Standards describe the SMP as the expertise that teachers should develop in their students. Unfortunately, low-income students of color are the least likely to engage in the behaviors outlined in the SMP. One way to ensure that all students have equitable access to powerful mathematics instruction is to ensure that they are taught in accordance with the SMP.

Students need to be taught the value of perseverance and productive struggle by engaging in meaningful, rich mathematical tasks. Teachers need to build students' abstract and quantitative reasoning by giving them problems in context that illustrate the relationships between quantities. When students construct viable arguments and critique each other's reasoning, they engage in meaningful discourse and dialogue. When students model with mathematics, they mathematize real-world situations that are important to them.

If students know when and how to use the correct tools, they will be better able to solve problems. Students who use repeated reasoning well are able to recognize and make sense of patterns. When students use precision in their calculations and language, they are better able to find and correct mistakes and explain their thinking. And when students make use of structure, they are able to generalize patterns that can be applied to new situations. Culturally relevant teaching is compatible with the SMP if teachers use tasks with contexts that come from the lived experiences of their students.

PERPETUATION OF INEQUITY ALONG RACIAL LINES

Everyone knows that inequity exists, but not everyone is willing to acknowledge it. Those who fail to be critically conscious or choose not to engage in culturally relevant teaching practices will continue to perpetuate inequity across racial and socioeconomic lines, whether it be consciously or unconsciously. Since teachers tend to teach in the same ways they were taught, a perpetuation of traditional mathematics teaching practices is inevitable unless a conscious effort is made to change. Playing the blame game often feels

safer than becoming self-reflective about the roles we play in repro-
ducing inequity in society. We are no exception. In this book, we
share stories that reflect our own inadequacies in hopes that it will
inspire and encourage you to reflect on your own practices.

Equity is a journey, not a destination. It will require constant
attention and vigilance. Because negative stereotypes spurred by racist ideology permeate every aspect of American society, an equity
framework can act as a lens for framing all of our education decisions. In the words of Gloria Ladson-Billings, it helps us to figure out
how to repay the educational debt that years of neglect and outright
hostility have produced.[2]

— QUESTIONS TO CONSIDER —

1. How might you educate yourself about the ways traditional
   mathematics instruction has perpetuated inequities along racial
   and economic lines?
2. Who can you get to join you in your quest to learn how to be a
   more equitable mathematics educator?

---

2   Gloria Ladson-Billings, "From the Achievement Gap to the Education Debt:
    Understanding Achievement in U.S. Schools," *Educational Researcher* 35, no. 7 (2006):
    3–12, https://thrive.arizona.edu/sites/default/files/From%20the%20Achievement%
    20Gap%20to%20the%20Education%20Debt_Understanding%20Achievement%20
    in%20US%20Schools.pdf.

CHAPTER ONE

INCLUDE OTHERS
AS EXPERTS

One day, students in my algebra class were working collaboratively on an assignment when two students, Deandre and Ashley,[1] began to argue loudly about who had the right answer to a problem. After hearing things like, "Why are you so dumb, Ashley?" and "Why are you so annoying, Deandre?" I decided to go over to their desks to help resolve their dispute. When I reviewed their work, I noticed Ashley had the correct answer, and without thinking it through, I told them this. Ashley shouted, "Now, who feels crunchy!" Deandre looked dejected and didn't immediately respond. I chastised Ashley for her insensitive response, but it was too late—the damage was done; Deandre had shut down.

Seeing Deandre's response, I instantly regretted how I had handled the situation. I was concerned that he would be much less likely to take mathematical risks in the future. Not only that, but Ashley was now mad at me for publicly reprimanding her. Additionally, by telling them who had the right answer, I had been the one to expend the most cognitive energy, robbing them of an opportunity to learn from each other. One spur-of-the-moment decision resulted in two disengaged learners! How

---

1   Pseudonyms are used throughout the book for students and teachers referenced in the narratives.

could I salvage this learning experience for Deandre and Ashley without sacrificing the academic needs.

When I took Deandre aside, I apologized to him for not handling the situation better. I reaffirmed to him our class values that mistakes are expected, respected, inspected, and corrected and that I appreciated his passionate engagement in class. I told him that the class needed his continued passion and expertise, and I pleaded for him to continue engaging with the class for the rest of the period. Then I spoke to Ashley. I first told her that I should not have reprimanded her in public and then asked her to think about how her actions had impacted Deandre. She said that she understood she'd hurt his feelings, and she apologized to him later. After this, they continued to work on the assignment in a much more respectful manner.

Pam

INCLUDE OTHERS AS EXPERTS

Create classroom environments that extend beyond the teacher as the sole authority to develop competence and confidence in others as experts, including the students themselves.

For many students, math class operates like a debate. Students who get the most correct answers are crowned the winners, while everyone else is a loser. Instead, math class should be more of a dialogue, an exchange of ideas where all parties seek both to understand and to be understood. That is the idea behind the principle of including others as experts.

We define experts as anyone who is able to contribute to the collective knowledge of the group. This principle encourages students to use whatever resources they have available to them to develop mathematical expertise. Culturally competent teachers urge students to look for expertise in their classmates, their families, and their communities.

INCLUDING OTHERS AS EXPERTS IS AN EQUITY ISSUE

A socially conscious teacher is aware that inequitable status interactions will inevitably occur—that is, unless they give students explicit instruction on how to effectively interact with each other during class. The story of Ashley and Deandre reminds us of the importance of redefining who the "experts" are in the room. Too often students view themselves and others through the lens of stereotypes. Students are more likely to give and receive help in class if the expertise of all students is emphasized, rather than the accomplishments of the few high-achieving "stars" in class. Inequity is perpetuated by the teacher when the same high-status students are consistently asked the "harder" questions because they are perceived as the experts. Inequity is perpetuated by students when they fail to seek the opinion of low-status students in class, even when they have expertise that can contribute to the knowledge of their classmates. Students who have internalized negative stereotypes about their math abilities are less confident in their own math abilities and less likely to see the expertise of others who look like them.

In an *Edutopia* article, mathematics educational specialist Joseph Manfre describes his Tiers of Understanding protocol that supports the principle of including others as experts in his math classroom.[2]

1. Tier 1: Do—Complete the task.
2. Tier 2: Explain the process to complete the task.
3. Tier 3: Empathetically explain the thought processes used by another student to complete the task.

---

2   Joseph Manfre, "How to Promote Productive Discussion in Math," *Edutopia*, March 27, 2020, https://www.edutopia.org/article/how-promote-productive-discussion-math.

    a. Listen to the other person.

    b. Try to see how they could be correct—maybe you're both correct. Math is not fixed, as there are many avenues to arrive at one solution, and solutions can appear in many equivalent forms.

    c. If you believe the other person is incorrect, explain how you are correct, and/or how they are incorrect. It is the responsibility of the person with the correct answer to rectify the misunderstanding.

Tier 1 helps students begin the process of developing their own expertise. Students who are not confident in their math abilities will often prefer for someone else to explain the process of solving the problem and may try to skip this step of solving the problem on their own. However, if students have not first had the opportunity to make sense of the problem for themselves, an explanation from someone else will still probably not be very helpful.

During Tier 2, students deepen their own understanding about the problem as they explain to their classmates how they thought about the problem. Unlike in traditional math classrooms, every student is responsible for sharing their thinking about the problem, not just those who are perceived as high status. Listening carefully to each other's explanations sets the foundation for the final step.

Tier 3 is where most of the cognitive work happens. When students have to explain their partner's thinking, their own understanding is deepened. This requires more critical thinking than just simply completing a problem. They have to think about whether they agree or disagree with their partner's process, what is similar and different about their processes, and whether different answers are the result of mistakes or misunderstandings. The level of cognitive demand required at this stage almost assures that learning will be more robust and retained longer. Teaching students how to empathetically explain thought processes can go a long way in avoiding the conflicts between students, like Ashley and Deandre. Once the class has gone through all three tiers, so much more expertise has been distributed across the class. The teacher has become just one of the many experts in the room!

Role of Perceived Competence

Whom do you ask for help when you struggle in math? Younger children naturally ask their parents. Parents who have a negative history with mathematics often pass on their own anxieties to their children when they try to help. One study even showed that the more time that math-anxious parents spent helping their children, the lower the math achievement was for the children.[3] Students who have parents with strong math skills or without math anxieties definitely have an advantage when seeking help from their parents. As children get older and the math gets harder, children tend to begin to rely more on their teachers for help. While this may happen naturally as students get acclimated to the more complex math topics in school, it can be more problematic as class sizes increase and every student expects their teachers to provide them one-on-one instruction whenever questions arise.

When the teacher is not available, students then have to determine whom to ask for help. This is where student perception of competence plays a role. Who is perceived as the smartest? Most likely, it is the students with the best grades or whomever the teacher praises most, those who are called on most frequently, or those who answer the teacher's questions with the most confidence.

In their study of classroom student interactions, Elizabeth Cohen and Rachel Lotan referred to these students as "high-status students." Low-status students were perceived to be less competent. Cohen and Lotan determined that the level of participation of students working collaboratively on open-ended tasks was more

3 Erin A. Maloney et al., "Intergenerational Effects of Parents' Math Anxiety on Children's Math Achievement and Anxiety," *Psychological Science* 26, no. 9 (2015): 1480–88, doi:10.1177/0956797615592630.

strongly impacted by race, ethnicity, and gender for low-status students than for high-status students.[4] What this means is that negative stereotypes associated with race, class, and gender are more likely to impact who is perceived as low status and, therefore, less competent. Because low-status students were observed to be less likely to talk, interact, and engage with their classmates while working in collaborative settings, the decreased academic achievement for those perceived as less competent should not be surprising.

Role of Confidence

Mathematics confidence can be defined as a student's perception of their ability to get good results in mathematics and their assurance that they can handle any mathematical difficulties they may face.[5] Students who have internalized negative stereotypes about their math abilities often lack confidence in mathematics. And those with low confidence also tend to be "nervous about learning new material, expect that all mathematics will be difficult, feel that they are naturally weak at mathematics, and worry more about mathematics than any other subject."[6]

Pam has a technique for spotting these students in her classroom. Like many teachers, she uses the first five minutes of class to take attendance and handle other administrative tasks while students quietly work on a review problem at their desks. When the

---

4 Elizabeth Cohen and Rachel Lotan, "Operation of Status in the Middle Grades: Recent Complications," in *Status, Network, & Structure: Theory Development in Group Processes*, ed. Jacek Szmatka, John Skvoretz, and Joseph Berger (Stanford, CA: Stanford University Press, 1997), 222–40.

5 Robyn Pierce and Kaye Stacey, "A Framework for Monitoring Progress and Planning Teaching towards the Effective Use of Computer Algebra Systems," *International Journal of Computers for Mathematical Learning* 9 (October 2004): 59–93, doi:10.1023B:IJCO.0000038246.98119.14.

6 Peter Galbraith and Christopher Haines, "Disentangling the Nexus: Attitudes to Mathematics and Technology in a Computer Learning Environment," *Educational Studies in Mathematics* 36, no. 3 (September 1998): 278, doi:10.1023/A:1003198120666.

timer goes off, they review the answer as a class. Pam had suspicions that many students were not doing these warm-up problems, so she decided to collect the work from each student each day. Pam noticed that some students consistently did not turn in their warm-up exercises, even though these problems were not being graded. It turned out, these were the same students who would not turn in their test papers, even though they appeared to be working on them. Other students would quickly copy what they saw written on a classmate's warm-up paper before turning in their own. These were the students who were determined to "hide" in Pam's class so that no one would find out they were "dumb" in math.

Students who lack confidence in mathematics often give up too quickly because they mistakenly believe that struggling means they are not smart (see our discussion on growth and fixed mindset in chapter 2 for more on this). Because they fear being exposed, they are less willing to voluntarily ask or answer questions. Even when they have followed the correct procedures, they will think their answers are wrong and erase them. They often do not take the time to check their answers against an answer key because they automatically assume they are wrong.

WHAT HAPPENS WHEN STUDENTS DON'T SEE THE EXPERTISE IN AND AROUND THEM

Culturally competent teachers understand that students frequently come to mathematics classrooms with internalized perceptions of who is mathematically smart. Racial, gender, and cultural stereotypes embedded in our society greatly influence those perceptions. When these negative stereotypes are paired with negative experiences in the mathematics classroom, students often conclude that they are unable to succeed in mathematics, or they may simply believe it's not worth the effort it takes to become successful. They may feel that putting their efforts into sports or entertainment will more likely produce results.

Similarly, students whose communities are viewed through a deficit lens will tend not to see community members as resources for academic help, especially when it comes to mathematics. These students see no connection between "school math" and the ways that their families and members of their community use mathematics on a daily basis. Many students feel that "real math" consists of worksheets full of repetitive exercises, as opposed to viewing math as noticing, describing, and generalizing patterns. Too often, the messiah complex makes teachers want to rescue students from their communities rather than see their communities as a resource for learning.

Students who don't believe they are good at math struggle in a multitude of ways. We have found that such students frequently exhibit the following characteristics:

- **They are more teacher dependent.** These students are the ones constantly calling the teacher over to validate their answers, asking, "Is this right?" They are less likely to make sense of a problem and persevere in solving it.

- **They are less likely to put forth the effort to build their own expertise.** When faced with learning something they perceive as hard, these students may avoid the task because they don't think they are capable.

- **They are more likely to doubt their own answers.** Students who lack confidence in their mathematical abilities are the ones who will erase their writing when you ask them a question about their answer because they assume if you are questioning it, it must be incorrect. If they reach a different answer than the "smart" students, they assume their answer is wrong.

- **They are less likely to ask peers for help.** For students who lack confidence, asking questions is not a sign of intelligence but rather an admission of ignorance. They are less likely to seek help from their peers because they fear exposing themselves and looking dumb.
- **They are more dependent on others to find their mistakes.** Rather than view making mistakes as a natural part of the learning process, students who lack confidence see mistakes as personal failures and are more likely to ignore them than address them. They tend to only address their mistakes when they are pointed out by others.
- **They are more likely to engage in negative self-talk when facing difficulty.** These are the students who will call themselves "stupid" when they can't understand a mathematical concept, get the answer to a problem incorrect, or aren't the first ones to get the correct answer.

OVERCOMING STUDENTS' LACK OF CONFIDENCE

It is extremely important that students experience mathematics in ways that help them see the mathematical expertise that resides in themselves, their classmates, their families, and their communities. Critically conscious teachers recognize that students generally only seek help from those they perceive as competent. They know that their job is to help students identify the mathematical expertise that lies within themselves and all around them and to teach them how to leverage this expertise to build their own confidence and competence in mathematics.

Researcher Megan Franke and her colleagues make the claim that students who have their problem-solving strategies explained to the class by their classmates benefit academically.[7] Research suggests this happens because teachers push students to further explain their thinking and compare their thinking with others'. When a student's problem-solving strategy is shared by another student, this raises the status of the student whose strategy was shared. Raising a student's status helps to build confidence. Having students share each other's strategies is also a way to have them include others as experts. In this section, we discuss some key strategies for helping students view themselves and others as experts.

Showing the value of building expertise

One strategy that has proven successful in getting students to understand the value of putting in hard work is to teach them about the concept of malleable intelligence, or the idea that the human brain is like a muscle: when you use it, it changes and gets stronger. Researchers at Columbia University conducted a study with two groups of seventh-grade students whose math scores had declined. Both groups of students participated in an eight-week study skills intervention. One group of students read articles about brain malleability, and the other group did not. The group that learned about brain malleability made remarkable improvements in their math scores, while the other group's scores continued to decline.[8]

To introduce this concept to students, teachers can provide lessons on malleable intelligence. (A link to sample lessons can be found in Appendix F.) Teachers can have students read articles and share what they found most surprising and interesting with their classmates. Students can also work in groups, with a group spokesperson

---

7   Noreen M. Webb, "Engaging with Others' Mathematical Ideas: Interrelationships among Student Participation, Teachers' Instructional Practices, and Learning," *International Journal of Educational Research* 63 (2014): 79–93, doi:10.1016/j. ijer.2013.02.001.

8   Society for Research in Child Development, "Students Who Believe Intelligence Can Be Developed Perform Better," *ScienceDaily*, February 7, 2007, www.sciencedaily.com/releases/2007/02/070207090949.htm.

sharing one example of brain malleability that they read about. Each group can then make a poster or PowerPoint presentation to share their information with the rest of the class. It is critical that teachers then continue to refer to these ideas throughout the school year to reinforce that students can learn if they are willing to put forth the effort.

Creating classrooms that inspire confidence

Look at whom your students ask for help. Who gets listened to and who gets dismissed? Students often view their textbooks and teachers as the only sources of knowledge in the mathematics classroom. However, as Gloria Ladson-Billings notes, "There is more expertise distributed across the classroom than there is in any one person."[9]

Traditional classrooms reinforce the idea that the teacher is the arbiter of knowledge who dispenses to those who dutifully follow their instructions. The culturally relevant teacher, however, does not view knowledge as static, but rather as continuously re-created and shared by both teacher and student. In this approach, teachers should look for opportunities where they can play the dual roles of student and co-teacher. One way of making a class less teachercentered is by striving to never say anything kids can say for themselves. That means allowing students to ask and answer their own questions, to respond to their classmates' questions, and to repeat and revoice others' thinking in their own words. Teachers redirect questions asked of them to other students.

This is where it is important to emphasize that the mathematics classroom is a learning community, where every student has a responsibility to learn and to contribute to the learning of their classmates. This is especially important for students who have internalized negative stereotypes about learning mathematics. Sometimes

---

9   Gloria Ladson-Billings, "V-FF. Gloria Ladson-Billings Cultural Competency," YouTube video, 3:10, posted by YouthWellness, January 22, 2012, https://www.youtube.com/watch?v=XSE8nxxZN5s.

students will do for others things they would not ordinarily do for themselves. The critically conscious teacher capitalizes on this idea to help build the learning community. Because low-status students will often avoid the appearance of looking dumb to their classmates, classroom structures that provide opportunities for them to contribute can invite otherwise reluctant learners to engage in meaningful mathematical activity.

One way to structure this interaction is by assigning roles to students working in mixed-ability groups. To support equal participation, group roles should be designed to be intellectually equal. Before assigning roles to students, the teacher should provide explicit instruction on each role. To include time for students to practice these roles during groupwork, we recommend that one role be introduced per week. Once the class has practiced all four roles, the teacher can communicate the expectation that these roles be used whenever group assignments are given in class. Teachers can assign roles at first and gradually turn that responsibility over to group members.

The following roles have been adapted from Cohen and Lotan's research complex instruction:[10]

- The **Coach** keeps the group together, making sure everyone's ideas are heard. They ask questions like, "Did anyone see it a different way?" and "Are we ready to move on?"
- The **Skeptic** helps students know they will need to provide justifications for their thinking and methods. They probe deeply into other students' processes, asking questions like, "How do you know that?" and "How does that relate to ...?"
- The **Accountability Manager** organizes the ideas of the group using mathematics principles, reasoning, and

---

10 Yekatarina Milvidskaia and Tiana Tebelman, "Rolling Out Group Roles," Google Docs, accessed January 2, 2021, https://docs.google.com/document/d/1-SA4eIG4oeQ_XPcy51ORVWEkHSb-5FzayLQZBmIuAdU/.

connections. They ask questions like, "How do we want to represent our ideas when it's time to meet with the teacher?"

- The **Team Captain** checks in with the team to see if they need any mathematical tools while solving a problem. They are the only one allowed to get up from the group to communicate with the teacher or members of other groups. They make sure that questions they ask outside the group can't be answered by any of the group members, and they have the responsibility of bringing any information from the teacher back to the group.

Another way students may try to avoid looking dumb to their peers is by not asking for help. It is important that teachers create classroom structures to help students overcome this fear, and one way to do this is by using instructional strategies that normalize seeking help. Find Someone Who, outlined below, is a *Kagan Cooperative Learning* strategy in which students are asked to find someone in the class who can explain to them how to work a problem on a worksheet.[11]

This activity helps students build confidence in their own and others' expertise in several ways. Since this activity requires everyone to ask for help, no one has to feel self-conscious about it. It also gives all students the chance to be teachers, as well as learners. This is especially important for low achievers who talk much less in class.[12] When students teach others, they remember approximately 90 percent of what they share. If teachers make themselves available to low-status students to explain how to work the hardest problems on the assignment, the low-status students can become the people from

---

11 Spencer Kagan and Miguel Kagan, *Kagan Cooperative Learning* (San Clemente, CA: Kagan Publishing, 2009).

12 Elizabeth Cohen and Rachel Lotan, "Producing Equal-Status Interaction in the Heterogeneous Classroom," *American Educational Research Journal* 32, no. 1 (1995): 99–120, doi:10.2307/1163215.

whom others have to get assistance. Seeing the boost in a student's confidence when they get to explain how to do one of the "hard" problems to the "smart" kids in the class is one of the great joys of teaching.

Find Someone Who

(Sample can be found in Appendix A.)

Setup: The teacher prepares a worksheet or set of questions for students.

Steps:

1. Students walk around the class, keeping a hand raised until they find a partner.

2. In pairs, Partner A asks a question from the worksheet; Partner B answers.

3. Partner A records the answer on his or her own worksheet, and Partner B checks and initials the answer.

4. Partners A and B switch roles and repeat steps 2 and 3, with Partner B asking and recording, and Partner A answering and checking.

5. Partners A and B part and raise a hand again as they each search for a new partner.

6. Students complete steps 1–5 until their worksheets are complete. They sit down when they are finished.

7. In their regularly assigned teams, students discuss answers. If there is disagreement or uncertainty, they all raise a hand to ask an agreed-upon team question.

Incorporating community stakeholders in mathematics instruction

Another way to emphasize collective knowledge is to include families and members of the community as part of the mathematics classroom, whether through assignments or service-learning opportunities or as guest speakers. In 2016, two organizations, TODOS: Mathematics for ALL and the National Council of Supervisors of Mathematics (NCSM), published a joint position statement on mathematics through the lens of social justice. Among the steps they recommended to implement social justice in math is partnering with families and communities. This includes learning about the knowledge, practices, and experiences of communities that can be used for mathematics lessons. It requires teachers and schools to create respectful, bidirectional feedback pathways with parents and caregivers.[13] Too often, the typical relationship of parents with the school is limited to participation in fund raisers or supervising students, and parents aren't seen as the important instructional resources they can be.

A valuable way of incorporating community stakeholders in mathematics instruction is through a Community Exploration Module. Developed by TEACH Math, a National Science Foundation–funded project aimed at helping new teachers teach effectively in communities that are economically and culturally diverse, the Community Exploration Module is focused on "knowledge of students' out of school activities and practices" and "engag[ing] in students' communities" and includes a community walk and the development of a mathematics lesson.

One example involved interviewing women in the community about the factors they consider when doing laundry. They found

---

13 TODOS, NCSM. "Mathematics Education through the Lens of Social Justice: Acknowledgment, Actions, and Accountability." (2016): https://www.todos-math.org/assets/docs2016/2016Enews/3.pospaper16_wtodos_8pp.pdf.

that, per week, the women averaged six to ten loads, depending on family size, and spent an average of fifteen to thirty dollars on laundry. Washing a load cost $1.75 for a single-load washer, $3.00 for a double-load washer, and $4.00 for a triple-load washer. The price for detergent was $0.75 per load, and the price to dry clothes was $0.25 for fifteen minutes.

Using this information, teachers were able to design the following lesson, which includes multistep operations, estimation, calculations with money, and comparing prices, for their third-grade students:

> Today your mother has 10 loads of laundry to do. She wants to know how much it will cost to wash (not dry) all of the clothes. Can you help her? How many solutions are there? What is the maximum and minimum you might pay if you already have the detergent?
>
> After the washing, now you and your mother have 10 loads of wet laundry. How much will it cost to dry all the loads? (Each load will need 45 minutes to dry on average).[14]

Community Exploration Modules illustrate the connection between school mathematics and the ways communities use math on a regular basis to solve real-world problems. By demonstrating that community members are engaging in complex mathematics in their everyday lives, Community Exploration Modules can help teachers change their beliefs about the communities they teach in and see the wealth of resources that reside within those communities to support their students' mathematical learning.

---

14 Corey Drake et al., "TeachMath Learning Modules for K–8 Mathematics Methods Courses," Teachers Empowered to Advance Change in Mathematics Project, 2015, http://www.teachmath.info.

Teaching self-assessment and self-correction

When teachers show students how to determine the correctness of their own answers, they support student self-efficacy by making them less dependent on their teacher. Critically conscious teachers don't just leave it up to students to figure out how to check their answers for accuracy; they explicitly teach them strategies to do so. For example, a teacher can teach elementary students to check the accuracy of $7 - 5 = 3$ by asking themselves, "Does $3 + 5 = 7$?" Realizing that $3 + 5 = 8$ and not 7, they know they have made an error. In the same way, students can check factoring by multiplying the factors.

A strategy Pam used was to purposefully assign students the odd problems in the textbook because the answers were in the back of the book. Sometimes, she would place answer keys underneath the desks or make each group's Team Captain the keeper of the key. She encouraged students to check their answers after each problem. If they got the same answer, they were most likely on the right track. If they had a different answer, then they had to ask themselves the following questions:

1. **Is my answer correct, but in a different form?** Students would check if their answers were mathematically equivalent or might need to be simplified.

2. **Did I make a mistake?** Students would evaluate their problems to see if they were set up properly and if the calculations were done correctly.

3. **Did I misunderstand something?** Students would be encouraged to get help in finding out what they misunderstood about the problem. This is where Pam implemented the routine of See Three Before Me. Students had to seek help from at least three other resources before seeking help from the teacher. For example, they could check their notes, check a book/online resource, and seek help from a classmate. If students still needed to come to her for help, she

would then be addressing the problem to multiple people at once, rather than answering the same question many times.

Providing students with context is another way teachers can help students learn to determine whether their answers are correct. For example, consider the following problem: 74 students need to go on a trip. How many cars will be needed if each car can carry 3 students? A student who divides 74 by 3 will get an answer of 24.666. Interpreting this answer in context would help the student realize that you can't have a third of a car, and therefore they would need to round up their answer to 25. Teachers who communicate the expectation that students write their answers to contextual problems using complete sentences and correct units are encouraging students to interpret their answers in the context of the problem.

When a student gets an answer that is incorrect, they have made an error. It is important to help students make a distinction between errors caused by mistakes and those caused by misunderstandings, since each requires a different course of action. Mistakes are made by accident by students who have an adequate understanding of the math. They can be corrected by the students themselves when they slow down, pay closer attention, or work more carefully. On the other hand, errors based on the misunderstanding of mathematical concepts or ideas cannot be self-corrected because the student is not aware of their misunderstanding. Sometimes students misinterpret presented information, have an incomplete understanding of the concepts, or have prior knowledge and/or experiences that contradict the information being presented. More practice will not overcome student misunderstandings. In fact, more often, it reinforces the misconception.

Because students are not even aware that they have misunderstandings, error analysis problems are a good way to uncover these misunderstandings. Error analysis involves giving students a problem that has been worked incorrectly based upon a common misunderstanding. Students are asked to find the error, explain why it is an error, and correct it. If these problems are completed in collaborative groups, students can rely on the expertise of fellow classmates to help them identify the errors. This way, misunderstandings that the teacher might not have the time to tackle can be addressed by fellow classmates. Mathmistakes.info is a good source for finding problems that can be used for error analysis.

One of the most powerful moves a teacher can make is changing the messages they give about errors, mistakes, and misunderstandings in mathematics. Brain research informs us that getting correct answers does not create the same type of brain growth and activity as when we make errors. Errors are not just opportunities for learning as students consider the errors; the cognitive dissonance that happens when students work problems that are beyond their current level of understanding generates increased brain activity even before a student knows whether their answer is correct or not. After receiving feedback, students who analyze and correct their errors create even more neural pathways in their brains, which makes learning easier and more enduring.[15] When we teach students that errors are positive, especially those based on misunderstandings, it has an incredibly liberating effect on them.

Jo Boaler, a professor in the Stanford Graduate School of Education, suggests the following strategies to celebrate making errors in the math classroom:[16]

1. At the beginning of the year, communicate to students that you absolutely love math errors!

2. Talk to students about why making errors is important to brain growth.

---

15 Jason S. Moser et al., "Mind Your Errors: Evidence for a Neural Mechanism Linking Growth Mind-set to Adaptive Posterror Adjustments," *Psychological Science* 22, no. 12 (2011), doi:10.1177/0956797611419520.

16 Jo Boaler, "Three Ways to Celebrate Mistakes in Class," PERTS Mindset Kit, https://www.mindsetkit.org/topics/celebrate-mistakes/3-ways-to-celebrate-mistakes-in-class.

3. Give students challenging work that encourages errors.

With these strategies, teachers can help change the ways students view errors. Teachers can use errors on assignments and assessments as opportunities to make sense of student thinking, such as analyzing student work to highlight your "favorite mistakes" that students made. This strategy is beautifully illustrated by eighth-grade math teacher Leah Alcala in a video on YouTube titled "My Favorite No."[17] If we want students to learn the value of errors, we need to give them challenging tasks accompanied by instructional support and positive messages about mistakes and errors. Remember that if students aren't making errors, they are not working at the right level.

Addressing negative-self talk

It is not enough that teachers recognize some students are approaching mathematics with a fixed mindset; critically conscious teachers actively work to support students in changing their mindsets when they find themselves falling into thought patterns that make them more likely to give up when they face obstacles to learning. Unfortunately, teachers using fixed mindset thinking can unwittingly reinforce this kind of negative approach by not interrogating their own thought processes and by blaming poor student performance on students' own fixed mindsets. Psychologist Carol Dweck addressed her concern about how her work was being misapplied in schools.[18] Rather than labeling students as having either a growth mindset or a fixed mindset, teachers should recognize that all of us have a combination of growth and fixed mindset thinking at different times in different areas. Dweck said that the goal is to help all students recognize their fixed mindset thinking when it occurs and

---

17 Leah Alcala, "My Favorite No," YouTube video, 3:02, posted by Maryland Formative Assessment, January 22, 2015, https://www.youtube.com/watch?v=uuDjke-p4Co.

18 Carol Dweck, "What Having a 'Growth Mindset' Actually Means," *Harvard Business Review,* January 13, 2016, https://hbr.org/2016/01/what-having-a-growth-mindset-actually-means.

develop counter-messages to these thoughts. For example, when a student answers a question incorrectly, she may think to herself, "I'm stupid." The critically conscious teacher normalizes those thoughts by publicly discussing them in class and sharing situations and times they've had them, too.

Pam definitely remembers having similar thoughts while sitting in her calculus courses at Georgia Tech and being totally confused during lectures. "You're not as smart as the rest of your classmates. They know more than you do because they are not struggling the way you are struggling." She also remembers countering those thoughts with, "Who can I ask to help me figure this out? I'll make sure I take good notes so we can discuss them when class is over."

Critically conscious teachers make addressing negative self-talk a normal part of the classroom experience. Wellness coach Elizabeth Scott makes the following recommendations for overcoming the negative conversations we have in our heads:[19]

- **Catch your inner critic and give it a name.** This strategy is about students seeing their inner critic as a force outside of themselves by giving it a name, like Sam. When they find themselves engaging in negative thoughts, they can say something like, "There goes Sam again trying to rain on my parade!"
- **Put limits on negativity.** Christian comedian Marcus D. Wiley played a fictitious religious character on the *Yolanda Adams Morning Show* named Bishop Secular, who regularly said that it was okay to be secular for two minutes.[20] Students could take on that same idea so that it's okay to be negative

---

19 Elizabeth Scott, "The Toxic Effects of Negative Self-Talk," *Very Well Mind*, February 25, 2020, https://www.verywellmind.com/negative-self-talk-and-how-it-affects-us-4161304.

20 Marcus D. Wiley, "Bishop Secular—Father's Day.wmv," YouTube video, 2:13, posted by 1MochaGirl1, June 19, 2011, https://www.youtube.com/watch?v=inTKbZ5OC3A.

for two minutes. After that, just like Elvis, Sam must leave the building!

- **Change the intensity of negative thoughts.** Sometimes it may be hard to shut the inner critic all the way down. It may be easier instead to change the intensity of negative language. For example, instead of saying, "I can't stand this class," you could say, "This class is challenging." "I hate math" instead becomes "Math is not my favorite subject."

- **Get it out of your head.** The problem with negative talk is that most times it goes unchallenged. Getting negative self-talk out of their heads by writing it down or speaking it aloud to someone else can really help students see how exaggerated or unrealistic it may be.

- **Out with the negative, in with the positive.** One of the best ways to combat negative self-talk is to replace it with something better. Below are a few examples.[21]

Instead of:	Try thinking:
I can't do this.	What am I missing?
I give up.	I'll use some of the strategies we've learned.
This is too hard.	This may take some time and effort.
I can't make this any better.	I can always improve, so I'll keep on trying.
I messed up.	Mistakes help me learn better.

---

21 Candice Naude, "Encouraging Students to Adopt a Growth Mindset," *Scooled! Teaching with Intent* (blog), August 14, 2014, https://scooled.wordpress.com/2014/08/24 /encouraging-students-to-adopt-a-growth-mindset/.

— QUESTIONS TO CONSIDER —

1. How are students in your classroom encouraged to view class-mates as experts?
2. In what ways are student views of who is an expert in the class based upon beliefs about race, class, or gender? How can you determine this?
3. How might you help students tap into the expertise that can be provided by members of their communities?

— CALL TO ACTION —

1. List the two ideas you learned from this chapter that are most relevant to your practice.
2. Complete the action plan on the following page for each idea.

Idea 1:

Vision for your students if you implement this idea in your classroom, school, or district	
Action step	
Deadline for action step	
Person you will ask to hold you accountable for completing this action step	

Idea 2:

Vision for your students if you implement this idea in your classroom, school, or district	
Action step	
Deadline for action step	
Person you will ask to hold you accountable for completing this action step	

CHAPTER TWO

BE CRITICALLY CONSCIOUS

I remember the first time I realized the impact of negative stereotypes. I was in eleventh grade and discussing SAT scores with one of my closest friends. She said to me, "You know the SAT is racist." When I asked her why she thought so, she responded, "Because they based those scores on White people, and we all know White people are smarter than us." I gave some kind of weak response about feeling that I was just as smart as any White person, and then I changed the subject.

But that conversation did not leave me. I was stunned and heartbroken my friend felt that way, and I wanted to know why. I also wondered how many other African American students in my South Carolina high school felt the same. Is that why there were so few other African American students in my honors-level courses? Even though I had all these thoughts rolling around in my head, at the time, I didn't know of anyone I felt safe enough to have these conversations with, so I kept those thoughts to myself.

— Pam

> ## BE CRITICALLY CONSCIOUS
>
> Being critically conscious means taking the time to under-stand how negative stereotypes impact diverse learners and actively working to erase the effects of these stereotypes on the educational outcomes of marginalized students.

The unfortunate reality of the history of this country is that groups of people have been discriminated against in systemic ways. Racism was an integral component of the educational systems that have evolved in the United States. This included the separation of students by race, racist depictions of people of color in curricular materials, and the under-resourcing of schools serving low-income students of color. Many of these racist policies were put in place due to stereotypes about the intellectual capabilities of people of color. Once in place, these policies persisted and are manifested for low-income students of color in outcomes like high failure rates, low grad-uation rates, the test score gap, and the school-to-prison pipeline.

If you are reading this book, we assume you are a well-intentioned person who only wants what's best for your students. But sometimes well-intentioned people do things that hurt others. Math teachers are no different. We want you to be prepared to realize that some of your well-intentioned math instructional practices may have actu-ally hurt some of your students academically. We understand what it feels like to find out that some of your practices have been ineffective for many and even traumatizing for some. We sincerely hope you are willing to take this journey with us as we share some of our real-izations, inspirations, failures, and celebrations. This journey begins with being critically conscious.

WHY CRITICAL CONSCIOUSNESS IS AN EQUITY ISSUE

Critical consciousness is about understanding how negative stereotypes impact student outcomes. Equity is focused on making sure all students receive the support they need to be successful. Negative stereotypes about students from marginalized groups create roadblocks to that success. In order to improve outcomes for marginalized students, teachers need to look beyond stereotypes and get to know who their students are as people and what their academic strengths and weaknesses are.

Achievement gap in mathematics

Everyone who has been involved in education for the last few decades has heard about the "achievement gap," or the difference in performance on standardized tests among different racial and ethnic groups. While there have been conferences convened and articles and books written on the topic, virtually nothing has caused the gap to decrease or disappear. But what's behind the data? What is the root cause of the difference in outcomes for different racial and ethnic groups?

UCLA's Institute for Democracy, Education, and Access (IDEA) identified three opportunity indicators that had a major impact on student performance in mathematics: class size, access to advanced mathematics courses, and access to qualified mathematics teachers.[1] We know that the fewer students a teacher has, the more likely it is they will be capable of meeting the needs of all of their students. IDEA found that high schools that had majority or predominantly Black, Latinx, and poor students had a higher percentage of mathematics classes with more than twenty-five students when compared with schools that were majority or predominantly White and Asian.

---

1   UC ACCORD and UCLA IDEA, "California Educational Opportunity Report 2007," https://idea.gseis.ucla.edu/publications/eor-07/StateEOR2007.pdf.

Students who intend to graduate high school and attend college need to take advanced mathematics courses. IDEA found that, in comparison with schools that were majority or predominantly White and Asian, a greater proportion of high schools that were majority or predominantly Black, Latinx, and poor enrolled less than 25 percent of students in advanced mathematics courses.

For a student to be successful in mathematics, they need teachers with a deep knowledge of the mathematics they are teaching, as well as an understanding of the best strategies to help students learn. On this point, IDEA found that a higher proportion of majority or predominantly Black, Latinx, and poor schools had severe shortages of qualified mathematics teachers than did majority or predominantly White and Asian schools.

Lastly, IDEA found that high schools that were majority or predominantly Black, Latinx, and poor were more than four times as likely to have all three of these opportunity problems as schools that were majority or predominantly White and Asian.[2]

Negative stereotypes of marginalized students

Just as young people are stereotyped in the larger society, they are also stereotyped as learners. In their book on equity in mathematics, *The Impact of Identity in K–8 Mathematics*, Julia Aguirre, Karen Mayfield-Ingram, and Danny Martin describe the types of negative stereotypes students of color are subject to that may hold them back from being successful mathematicians and recommend that teachers take responsibility for developing positive mathematics identities in all of their students. To do this successfully, teachers must move away from negative stereotypes. For example, if a teacher buys into the stereotype of Black males as "thugs," the teacher might fail to hold Black male students accountable for participation for fear the students may disrupt the classroom. Likewise, if a teacher stereotypes

2   Ibid.

Latinx and Asian children as "illegal aliens" or "anchor babies," they might assume that they don't speak English or have not had formal schooling. Teachers need to avoid reducing children to nameless, objectified data points (as "bubble kids," those students who are only a few points away from scoring proficient on standardized tests, for instance) in larger conversations about assessment.[3]

An activity that Kyndall has used in professional development to help teachers recognize the impact of negative stereotypes is called What Have You Heard? The activity was developed by Dr. Julia Aguirre at the University of Washington, Tacoma.[4] In this activity, posters are placed around the room with the names of different groups of students on them, such as "Black boys," "Asian youth," "Latinx students," or "Poor students." Teachers are then given the task of visiting each poster and writing comments they have heard about these groups of students from other educators or the general public, whether they believe them to be true or not. After everyone has had an opportunity to add comments to the posters, groups of four to five teachers take one of the posters and sort the comments.

When this activity was done at a national equity conference, the statements on the posters were categorized as positive, negative, or neutral. On the poster for Black boys, 7 percent of the statements were positive (e.g., "They tend to like to find their own way to solve a problem."), and 93 percent were negative ("They don't have the basic skills to learn math."). On the poster for Latinx students, 18 percent were positive ("They know more math because they already learned it in Mexico."), while 78 percent were negative ("They can't learn math if they don't speak the language.") and 4 percent were neutral ("Latinx students are ELL."). Although these statements were not necessarily something the teachers who wrote them agreed with,

---

3 Julia Aguirre, Danny Martin, and Karen Mayfield-Ingram, *The Impact of Identity in K-8 Mathematics: Rethinking Equity-Based Practices* (Reston, VA: National Council of Teachers of Mathematics, 2013).

4 Julia Aguirre, personal conversation, June 29, 2016.

they were pretty consistent with those written when this activity is replicated in different venues around the country, indicating that these kinds of stereotypes are pervasive.

Indeed, such stereotypes have found their way into major mathematics education research, as well as policy documents. In its findings on learning processes, the 2008 Final Report of the National Mathematics Advisory Panel from the US Department of Education says:

> Unfortunately, most children from low-income backgrounds enter school with far less knowledge than peers from middle-income backgrounds, and the achievement gap in mathematical knowledge progressively widens throughout their PreK–12 years.[5]

The Second Handbook of Research on Mathematics Teaching and Learning from the National Council of Teachers of Mathematics (NCTM) characterizes low-income students in a similar fashion:

> Although low-income children have pre-mathematical knowledge, they do lack important components of mathematical knowledge. They lack the ability—because they have been provided less support to learn—to connect their informal pre-mathematical knowledge to school mathematics.[6]

When teachers buy into the negative stereotypes about students of color that are projected in the media and research, they are likely to have lower expectations for these students. And when they have low expectations of students, they are less inclined to engage them in high-level, cognitively demanding mathematics tasks. Teachers need

---

5   US Department of Education, "The Final Report of the National Mathematics Advisory Panel 2008," https://www2.ed.gov/about/bdscomm/list/mathpanel/report /final-report.pdf.

6   National Council of Teachers of Mathematics, *The Second Handbook of Research on Mathematics Teaching and Learning*, ed. Frank Lester (Reston, VA: NCTM, 2007).

to put aside their preconceived notions of students, see them for who they are, and recognize their academic potential.

WHAT HAPPENS IF WE ARE NOT CRITICALLY CONSCIOUS

If teachers are not critically conscious, then students from marginalized groups will continue to experience the effects of negative stereotypes on their educational outcomes. Sociologists and psychologists have categorized the effects of these negative stereotypes as follows: stereotype threat, internalization of negative stereotypes, and decreased interest in studying mathematics.

Stereotype threat

When exposed to the threat of being evaluated, judged, or treated in terms of a negative stereotype about a group to which they belong, individuals can perform worse than they would have in a domain in which these stereotypes do not exist. More than three hundred studies have shown that, in clinical settings, when students are subjected to negative stereotypes about a group to which they belong, it can trigger anxieties that result in significantly worse performance, even if they don't believe the stereotype. For example, the psychologist Claude Steele conducted a series of studies where two groups of students that had been selected based on similar academic characteristics were given the same test. Only the treatment group was told that the test measured academic ability. The African American students in this group scored significantly lower than the African American students in the control group. Similar results occurred around other stereotyped groups, such as women scoring lower than men, and White males scoring lower than Asian males on math tests. According to Steele, this phenomenon, referred to as "stereotype threat," even applied to nonacademic stereotypes, such as

White males in the treatment group performing significantly lower than the White males in the control group when they were told the test measured their athletic abilities. So, for example, if African American students have been exposed to the stereotype that African Americans don't do well on standardized tests, it may cause them to underperform on such tests.

Internalization of negative stereotypes

Stereotype threat can impact students during specific events, whether or not they believe the stereotype. Internalization of negative stereotypes is more debilitating because, over time, they become self-fulfilling prophecies. A study published in 2017 confirms the idea that students who believe the system is fair are more susceptible to believing negative stereotypes as they get older.[7] Researchers asked students in urban middle schools in Arizona to rate themselves in terms of self-esteem, participation in risky behaviors, and perceived fairness of society. In sixth grade, believing that the system was fair and just was actually associated with higher self-esteem and less risky behavior. However, these same beliefs predicted a decline in self-esteem and an increase in risky behavior as these sixth graders moved through seventh and eighth grades. In other words, while belief in a fair system was a benefit to marginalized students in the sixth grade, that belief became a liability as they got older.

Erin Godfrey, the lead researcher of the study, describes this phenomenon as "system justification." System justification is the theory that people tend to defend the status quo because they believe that the overarching social, economic, and political systems are fair and legitimate. It is built on myths like, "If you just work hard enough,

---

7   Erin Godfrey, Carlos Santos, and Esther Burson, "For Better or Worse? System-Justifying Beliefs in Sixth-Grade Predict Trajectories of Self-Esteem and Behavior Across Early Adolescence," *Child Development* 90, no. 1 (June 2017): 180–95, doi:10.1111/cdev.12854.

you can pull yourself up by your bootstraps" or "Success is just a matter of motivation and talent and grit."

An explanation for why this pattern shows up in middle school is that early adolescence is a time of rapid cognitive development, allowing students to think more abstractly about larger societal systems. It is a time where marginalized youth are gaining a more complex understanding of institutionalized discrimination at the same time that they are solidifying their social identifies as members of a racial or ethnic group. For youth who have an advantaged position in society, believing that anyone can be successful through hard work and talent doesn't create any internal conflict because they can feel good about how they've "made it." However, Black, Latinx, and low socioeconomic status youth are often stereotyped as "aggressive" and "delinquent," and they frequently experience discrimination based on these stereotypes (e.g., being followed in a store or stopped by the police). As marginalized students become more aware of the inequities in the system, they may begin to wonder what is wrong with them or with their social group. They may think, "If the system is fair, why am I seeing that everybody who has brown skin is in this kind of job?" This internal conflict leads to disillusionment and may lead these students to think, "Since people already believe this about me, I might as well act like it." It is critically important to actively address the impacts of negative stereotypes on marginalized youth, especially in early adolescence when this dissonance begins to deepen.

Decreased interest in studying mathematics

Negative stereotypes also lead students to believe they are unable to succeed at mathematics. As a result, they are often discouraged from pursuing math-related fields and instead encouraged to engage in sports, music, or the arts. This is reflected in the fact that, although African Americans are 13.4 percent of the US population, they received only 9 percent of all science and engineering bachelor's degrees in 2016.[8]

Between 2000 and 2010, STEM-related jobs grew at three times the rate of non-STEM-related jobs, and in 2018, 2.4 million STEM jobs went unfilled. Because people of color are underrepresented in STEM disciplines, many lack the qualifications to access these jobs, which on average pay a higher rate than non-STEM-related jobs, with the result that fewer African Americans pursue STEM-related jobs.[9] Only 6 percent of the STEM workforce in 2018 was Black.[10]

OVERCOMING NEGATIVE STEREOTYPES THROUGH CRITICAL CONSCIOUSNESS

Being critically conscious is a way to help teachers reject negative stereotypes. It means understanding that a student's race is a part of their identity that needs to be acknowledged and not ignored. Being critically conscious also involves investigating prejudices that individuals have within themselves and those that are part of the systems they work in.

Be color-conscious, not color-blind

Because racism is such a difficult topic for many teachers, some will say, "I don't see race. I only see students." This "color-blindness" is a thinly veiled attempt to avoid the discomfort of discussing issues of race in a meaningful way. While this statement is intended to

---

8 "Women, Minorities, and Persons with Disabilities in Science and Engineering," National Science Foundation, https://ncses.nsf.gov/pubs/nsf19304/digest/about-this-report.

9 Ibid.

10 National Science Board, "Science and Engineering Indicators 2018," National Science Foundation, https://nsf.gov/statistics/2018/nsb20181/report/sections/science-and-engineering-labor-force/women-and-minorities-in-the-s-e-workforce#minorities-in-the-s-e-workforce.

communicate a lack of bias, it is actually offensive. Because being Black is such a big part of our identity, when we hear people say they don't see color, what we actually hear is, "I don't want to acknowledge your Blackness because it makes me uncomfortable." The fact that a person had to go out of his way to say that he doesn't notice a physical attribute infers that this attribute is not normal or that something is wrong with it. I have never heard anyone say, "I don't see hair color" or "I don't see eye color." People obviously see hair color, eye color, skin color, and a host of other physical characteristics, and when people feel the need to state that they don't see an obvious physical trait, it is much more of an indication of attitudes and beliefs about race they are trying to hide than a positive statement about their supposed lack of prejudice.

Critically conscious teachers cannot be color-blind. When teachers fail to take students' race or culture into consideration when making pedagogical decisions, the dominant culture of the teacher becomes the only one valued or "seen" in the classroom to the detriment of those who are not members of that cultural group.[11] Critically unconscious teachers will not be able to understand the impact of negative stereotypes on their students. Rather than hiding their own biases by avoiding conversations about race, critically conscious teachers must reflect on their own personal biases. This personal reflection very rarely happens apart from meaningful dialogue with others about issues of race.

Tina's Story

I've seen on social media and even heard people I know say, "I don't see the color of a person's skin." I know I've said it silently in my head. In education [Tina is an elementary education consultant], we use this phrase with the best of intentions—we want people to know that we love our students, no

---

11 Norma C. Presmeg, "Ethnomathematics in Teacher Education," *Journal of Mathematics Teacher Education* 1, no. 3 (1998): 317–39.

matter the color of their skin—but I didn't realize the harmful impact of color-blindness until an interaction with one of my friends.

I have a group of friends who have all known each other since we were in elementary school. We communicate every day in a group video chat app. We all grew up in the same small town, and all of us except one are White.

Renee went to school with us in elementary school, moved away, then came back in high school. She was my matron of honor in my wedding. She is also part Black, and I've never once asked her about her race or racism.

In the time of George Floyd, Ahmaud Arbery, and the protests against racial injustice, I finally realized something I never had before: one of my best friends could be in danger just because of the color of her skin.

During one of our regular group chats, I asked Renee if she ever experienced racism. I asked her to share her experiences with the group if she felt comfortable doing so. I also apologized for never asking her in the over thirty years we've known each other.

After she had shared her stories, another friend in the group thanked her and apologized for never having asked her about her experiences either. And she made a comment that stuck with me: She said she hadn't ever asked because Renee just always seemed like "one of us." She didn't see Renee as different.

Because we didn't acknowledge Renee's differences, we'd never been there to help her navigate them or the experiences they have brought her. Our color-blindness had kept us from learning about everything that makes Renee, Renee.

After this interaction, I happened to watch a video by Dr. Robin DiAngelo, the author of White Fragility, in which she discussed this very issue. She talks about the difference between those who are "color-blind" and those who are "color-celebrate." When we say that we "don't see color," we are negating a person, their heritage, their experiences, and on and on. Instead, we need to recognize and honor color. We need to do this for the people in our lives, and we need to do it for the students in our classrooms.

Examine your own biases

In her book, *Why Are All the Black Kids Sitting Together in the Cafeteria? And Other Conversations about Race*, psychologist Beverly Tatum asserts that everyone has prejudices because everyone is continually exposed to misinformation about others through stereotypes, omissions, and distortions.[12] She likens prejudice to smog, an inescapable consequence of living in a racist society. While sometimes it is so thick it can be seen and other times it is invisible, people breathe it in and out every day—not because they want to, but because it is the only air available.

Tatum extends the metaphor by explaining that people do not introduce themselves as "smog-breathers," in the same way they do not want to be identified as prejudiced. Still, if a person lives in a "smoggy" place, constantly bombarded by stereotypes and misinformation, they cannot avoid breathing the air. No one is completely free of prejudices, even people of color. They breathe the same polluted air and often internalize these stereotypes to some degree. Although, Tatum says, prejudice is part of a person's socialization and thus not their fault, just because someone may not have polluted the air doesn't mean it isn't their responsibility to clean it up. Each person must examine their own behavior. Unless people commit to actively examining and challenging their own prejudices, they will be guilty of perpetuating and reinforcing the negative messages so pervasive in society. Critically conscious teachers, therefore, constantly reflect on how their interactions with students either reinforce or challenge these messages.

One activity we have used to help teachers rethink the existing negative stereotypes about learners is to reframe these stereotypes. As part of the What Have You Heard? activity described earlier, once teachers have sorted and analyzed the statements about different learners, we ask them to look at the statements that use deficit

---

12 Beverly Tatum, *Why Are All the Black Kids Sitting Together in the Cafeteria? And Other Conversations about Race* (New York: Basic Books, 1997).

language and rewrite them using asset-based language. For example, "Black boys don't have the basic skills to learn math" could be rewritten as "Black boys use basic skills in everyday activities like shopping, games, or cooking." The statement "Latinx students can't learn math if they don't speak the language" could be rewritten to say "Bilingualism is a tool to help students learn mathematics." Such activities help teachers become more sensitive to the language they use to characterize student behavior and performance.

Be aware of how negative stereotypes impact student interactions

Critically conscious teachers not only reflect on their own actions, they also give attention to the interactions and policies that exist within school structures that lead to negative educational outcomes for Black, Brown, and poor children. They continually take notice of how students interact with each other in the classroom and of the status distinctions students make along racial, gender, and socioeconomic lines. Negative stereotypes about the inferior intellectual capacities of students of color often play out in the mathematics classroom. Because mathematics tends to be perceived as difficult, these negative stereotypes contribute to the social status, expert status, academic status, and peer status attributed to students. Further contributing to unequal status interactions is the idea that mathematics ability is static, genetic, and/or innate. Members of negatively stereotyped groups will more likely be perceived as incompetent or incapable when they make mistakes in class.

Because one's learning is dependent upon the ability to reflect on, discuss, and meaningfully engage with information, students who feel they have a lower status within the group will be at a great disadvantage. For example, because of previous experiences of being dismissed, ridiculed, or ignored, some students are hesitant to speak up in class, even though their ideas may be valid. They may choose to sit back and play a passive role in the classroom, learning less than if they had engaged in more meaningful interactions around the content with their classmates. Conversely, high-status students will be more likely to be actively engaged with their peers, giving them many opportunities to learn. Critically conscious teachers understand that if they do not actively intervene to disrupt them, these unequal status interactions will continue to impair the learning of low-status students.

COMBATING NEGATIVE STEREOTYPES

Being aware of negative stereotypes and their impacts on marginalized students is not sufficient to effect change. Critically conscious teachers must become advocates for change in their classrooms, schools, and communities.

Assigning competence

There are many ways critically conscious teachers have actively worked to erase the effects of negative stereotypes on their students. One such strategy is assigning competence. In her book, *Designing Groupwork*, Elizabeth Cohen defines assigning competence as "the form of praise where teachers catch students being smart."[13] With this technique, teachers use their power to bring attention to the strengths of students who are often perceived as having low social status within the mathematics classroom (i.e., African American and Hispanic students, special education students, or students with low socioeconomic backgrounds). Below, we outline the steps to assigning competence to the students in your classroom:

1. Identify a group-worthy task, one that requires sensemaking, has multiple entry points, and an engaging context.

---

13 Elizabeth Cohen and Rachel Lotan, *Designing Groupwork: Strategies for the Heterogeneous Classroom,* 3rd ed. (New York: Teachers College Press, 2014).

2. Work the task yourself, and then brainstorm a list of mathematical abilities necessary to complete it, such as seeing visual patterns, asking questions of the group to get all ideas out on the table, and making connections between different methods.

3. Create a checklist (see Appendix B) that includes the names of your students and lists the mathematical abilities you and your students identified in the previous step.

4. Now have students work the task while you observe the social interactions in the classroom. Who speaks up the most? Who is asked the most questions? Who is listened to most often? Who rarely says anything? Who has their ideas shot down or dismissed?

5. Record notes about students' strengths as they engage with the task. Note that you cannot do this step if you are busy helping students. Tell your scholars that you are unavailable and to instead use each other as resources.

6. Take every opportunity to elevate the status of low-status students by genuinely pointing out their successes publicly. For example, "Javier, I see that you noticed a pattern and represented it with a great visual model. Can you tell us about your thinking when you made your diagram?" It is important for the praise to be public, intellectually meaningful, and specific to the task.

7. When conferencing with students about their academic progress, share your checklist of their mathematical abilities that have been recorded over time so they can see the progress they have made.

Growth mindset

Another way critically conscious teachers intervene to disrupt stereotypes and unequal status treatments is to implement a growth mindset classroom. A growth mindset is the idea that intelligence is malleable and that the way to become smarter is by doing challenging work. Compare this to a fixed mindset view of intelligence, whereby some people are naturally smart, others are not, and these capabilities remain static. If academic tasks are easy for you, it must mean that you are smart; if you are having difficulty, it must mean you have reached the limits of your intelligence and, further, you must hide this fact from others at all costs. The result is that students avoid engaging in the very behaviors that will help them be successful in mathematics. To a person with a fixed mindset, there is no such thing as productive struggle—the very fact that you struggle is proof you can't do it. When you add negative stereotypes about intellectual ability into the mix, you can see how the ramifications of having a fixed mindset can be especially damaging for students from marginalized groups.

Unfortunately, traditional school structures in the United States reinforce a fixed mindset. The typical grading system reaffirms that smart kids are the ones who make As and Bs and that students who make Ds and Fs are dumb. Standardized testing where students are labeled level 1–4 based upon their performance on a single test also often supports a fixed mindset. When teachers themselves have successfully matriculated through these traditional systems, a fixed mindset becomes the default when they lead their own classrooms.

With this understanding in mind, critically conscious teachers must first examine their own ideas about whether students are naturally smart in math or whether their abilities can grow as a result of time, effort, and implementation of effective strategies. Second, critically conscious teachers reflect on their classroom practices and how these practices reinforce either a growth or fixed mindset. For example, when a student performs poorly on a unit test, typically that grade is recorded in the grade book, and students don't see that content again until the end of the year. Instead of just moving on, critically conscious teachers ask themselves, "How can I encourage those who performed well to continue learning? How can I encourage my fixed mindset students to put forth the effort necessary to learn from their mistakes? How can I help them find and apply more effective strategies to learn this content? Does my system of rewards only recognize high achievement or does it honor growth as well?" These teachers constantly adjust their practice to answer these questions and make sure their classrooms support and encourage a growth mindset in their students. Psychologist Carol Dweck, who pioneered the concepts of fixed and growth mindsets, says, "I tell students, 'You are quitting your old job and starting your new job. Your old job was getting as many As as possible. Your new job is to use all the resources . . . to become the person you want to be, and to contribute something important to the world.'"[14]

An often-overlooked aspect of growth mindset is a teacher's beliefs when it comes to their own teaching abilities. Too often teachers who have a growth mindset when it comes to learning mathematics can fall into a fixed mindset when it comes to addressing challenges in the classroom. When students do not meet the teacher's academic expectations, rather than focusing on their own mistakes or learning more effective strategies to meet the needs of their students, teachers with fixed mindsets blame their students or focus on things beyond their control (e.g., family support outside of school or what students learned from a previous teacher). The critically conscious teacher is careful to focus on learning from their mistakes and on developing more effective strategies to avoid falling into a fixed mindset when students perform poorly.

The ways that we provide feedback to students can have an impact on their mindsets as well. Kyndall recalls, "I can remember when I was a student getting tests back from my mathematics

14 Sarah D. Sparks, "Building Growth Mindset in the Classroom: Assignments from Carol Dweck," *Education Week*, May 28, 2019, https://www.edweek.org/leadership/building-growth-mindset-in-the-classroom-assignments-from-carol-dweck/2019/05?cmp=eml-eb-mindset-recur.v5.

teachers with red Cs for the problems I got correct and red Xs for the problems I got incorrect. There was a fraction written near the top of the paper with the number of problems I got correct in the numerator and the total number of problems on the test in the denominator. I don't remember a mathematics teacher ever giving me authentic feedback explaining what I did correctly or incorrectly."

David Yeager and his colleagues studied what happens when you provide students with "wise feedback," a strategy of building trust with students by expressing a belief that they are capable of meeting high standards. Yeager and his colleagues found that when teachers provided feedback to African American students followed by the statement, "I am giving you these comments because I have very high expectations and I know that you can reach them," 64 percent of the students revised their assignment as opposed to only 27 percent who did not receive the wise feedback.[15]

Mathematics teachers need to do a better job providing students with feedback on assessments. Teachers need to explain to students what they did correctly, acknowledge partial understandings on problems they did incorrectly, and give them opportunities to revise problems they answered incorrectly. These practices, coupled with wise feedback, have the potential to increase the agency of African American students.

Negative stereotypes about students from marginalized groups most often result in unconscious biases that influence virtually every instructional decision we make in and out of the mathematics classroom. We will spend the rest of this book unpacking some of those influences.

---

15 David Yeager et al., "Breaking the Cycle of Mistrust: Wise Interventions to Provide Critical Feedback across the Racial Divide," *Journal of Experimental Psychology: General* 143, no. 2 (2014): 804–24, doi:10.103710033906.

— QUESTIONS TO CONSIDER —

1. How do negative stereotypes influence your interactions with low-status students?
2. How do you make sure that all of your students—both high and low status—participate equally during whole group and small group instruction?
3. Who are the low-status students in your class? What strategies can you use to assign competence to them?

— CALL TO ACTION —

1. List the two ideas you learned from this chapter that are most relevant to your practice.
2. Complete the action plan below for each idea.

Idea 1:	
Vision for your students if you implement this idea in your classroom, school, or district	
Action step	
Deadline for action step	
Person you will ask to hold you accountable for completing this action step	

Idea 2:	
Vision for your students if you implement this idea in your classroom, school, or district	
Action step	
Deadline for action step	
Person you will ask to hold you accountable for completing this action step	

CHAPTER THREE

UNDERSTAND YOUR STUDENTS WELL

As a freshman, Morgan failed every test, often spoke about how bad she was at math, and rarely completed her class assignments. Although she was always pleasant in class, she was frequently absent. When I saw Morgan's name on my algebra II roster a few years later, I wondered if Morgan would be willing to work harder than she had as a freshman. This time I asked my students to tell me their math stories at the beginning of the semester. After learning Morgan's math story (which will be shared later in this chapter), I felt remorse for not doing enough to reach out to her and was embarrassed by the many assumptions that I had made about her. I had only known Morgan as an unmotivated ninth grader who hated math. But if I had asked her to tell her story when she was in algebra I, I might have gotten to know the Morgan who had loved math and enjoyed teaching her classmates multiplication. I would have worked harder to help her connect to her previous positive math experiences. Although I may regret that I can never know how my interactions with students might have been different if I had known about their histories with math, all I can do is learn from my mistakes and commit to doing better moving forward. That is why I now ask my students to share their math stories at both the beginning and end of the year.

— *Pam* —

UNDERSTAND YOUR STUDENTS WELL

Learn about your students, their families, and their communities for the purpose of improving instruction (not making assumptions).

Assumptions are usually constructed from stereotypes. Instead of buying into preconceived notions of students based upon their racial and ethnic backgrounds, their grades, or their test scores, teachers need to respect their students enough to take the time to find out who they are as people. Teachers can use a variety of strategies to find out their students' backgrounds and personal interests and then use that information to build classroom community and design lessons.

Assumptions about students from marginalized groups are often negative. To best prepare our students for an unknown future, we need to know them as human beings—human beings who have aspirations for their future, who have hopes, and who also have fears. If we don't see them in their humanity, we will be tempted to instead see them as numbers, as statistics, as their labels (e.g., low level, urban, at-risk, special ed, ELL, underperforming). When we don't see them in their humanity, we fail to see how our interactions might dash their hopes and exacerbate their fears.

As Patricia, a high school mathematics teacher, says, "I think for me, my role as a teacher is to get to know the kids for who they are, and know what their interests are, and know how they learn, and then once I know that, then I can incorporate all those different things in my lessons to address all the different students that I have."[1]

---

1   Pamela Seda, "Equity Pedagogy in the Secondary Mathematics Classrooms of Three Preservice Teachers" (PhD dissertation, Georgia State University, 2008), 83.

WHY UNDERSTANDING YOUR STUDENTS IS AN EQUITY ISSUE

When we understand our students well, we see beyond their labels and beyond the statistics to the variety of talents, strengths, and skills we might be able to draw upon to make mathematical connections and improve instruction. This means seeing their communities, their families, their cultural traditions, and their extracurricular activities all as potential reservoirs for these connections and improvements. Understanding your students is about intentionally looking beyond what you typically see in a math classroom, like homework, tests, raised hands, or unanswered questions, to notice the things that motivate, bring joy to, and intrigue your students, so you can leverage them in the math classroom. It may include tailoring the contexts for your problems to something your students have experience with, such as providing grocery store contexts because you know some of your students regularly do the family's grocery shopping. Most important, it means moving beyond the stereotypes about students from marginalized groups and taking the time to know who they are beyond the mathematics classroom because what you might learn can help you become a better mathematics teacher for all of your students.

Dehumanizing effects of negative stereotypes

One result of negative stereotyping is the "adultification" of Black children. In a study about the effects of the dehumanization of Black children, researchers studied how a group of students at a large university perceived the "innocence" of children from different racial and ethnic groups. They found that Black children were seen as less innocent than White children. More specifically, after the age of ten, Black children are seen as significantly less innocent than children of any other age group. The perceived innocence of Black children aged ten to thirteen was equivalent to that of non-

Black children aged fourteen to seventeen. The perceived innocence of Black children aged fourteen to seventeen was equivalent to that of non-Black adults aged eighteen to twenty-one. The researchers concluded that Black children are more likely to be prematurely regarded as similar to adults.[2] The attitudes described here often find their way into classrooms and impact the ways that teachers think and feel about Black students. These findings are consistent with the way that Black girls, in particular, are perceived.

> Black girls are often stereotyped as talkative, loud, confrontational and assertive. . . . Therefore, teachers assume Black girls need more social correction, and more emphasis is placed on social correction than on academic development and achievement.[3]

Assumptions about the innocence or maturity level of Black children inevitably result when teachers do not take the time to understand who their students truly are. These assumptions cause teachers to wrongly judge students and make instructional decisions that are detrimental to their success in mathematics.

When teachers perceive students as innocent, they react differently to regular classroom interactions. They tend to be more gracious toward the behavior of students whom they perceive to be more innocent. For example, when a student who is perceived as innocent fails to turn in an assignment, teachers are more willing to give that student some leeway, such as more time to turn it in. However, when a student who is perceived as not innocent fails to turn in an assignment, the response is more punitive (e.g., no credit, no late turn in, or a failing grade). Teachers are more likely to respond positively to

---

2 Philip Atiba Goff et al., "The Essence of Innocence: Consequences of Dehumanizing Black Children," *Journal of Personal and Social Psychology* 106, no. 4 (2014): 526–45.

3 Crystal Morton and Demetrice Smith-Mutegi, "Girls STEM Institute: Transforming and Empowering Black Girls in Mathematics through STEM," in *Rehumanizing Mathematics for Black, Indigenous, and Latin@/x Students* (Reston, VA: NCTM, 2018), 24.

the questions of students they perceive as innocent as opposed to those they do not perceive as innocent.

How you interpret and respond to student behavior is often influenced by negative stereotypes. Dan Battey and his colleagues at Rutgers University studied twenty-five middle school mathematics classrooms that were either predominately Black or predominately White. They found that "White teachers in predominately Black schools were more likely than White teachers in predominately White schools to respond in negative ways to student behavior, emotions, and ability."[4]

Math anxiety and math trauma

For many students, math classes are places of anxiety, pain, and trauma. Because of the ramifications of negative stereotypes, this is especially true for students who are female, from low-income families, or non-White.[5] Math anxiety is a feeling of tension, apprehension, or fear that interferes with math performance. Research shows that negativity actually hinders the brain's ability to engage in critical thinking and problem solving. Teachers who don't understand the role math anxiety plays in learning may mistakenly assume students are unmotivated or unwilling to learn. Students from marginalized groups are more often stigmatized by these assumptions when teachers operate on their unconscious biases rather than taking the time to really understand their students.

Closely related to math anxiety is math trauma. "Math trauma stems from an event, a series of events, or a set of circumstances experienced by an individual as harmful or threatening such that there are lasting adverse effects on the individual's functioning and

---

4 Dan Battey et al., "Racial (Mis)Match in Middle School Mathematics Classrooms: Relational Interactions as a Racialized Mechanism," *Harvard Educational Review* 88, no. 4 (2018): 455.

5 Kasi Allen, "Math Trauma: Healing Our Students, Our Classrooms, and Our Discipline," webinar, April 5, 2016, https://www.bigmarker.com/GlobalMathDept/Math-Trauma -Healing-Our-Classrooms-Our-Students-and-Our-Discipline.

well-being in the perceived presence of mathematics."[6] Unlike math anxiety, which is based on an individual's feelings or mindset, math trauma results from external events that are stressful and shatter a person's sense of security, contributing to feelings of helplessness and vulnerability. These traumatic events can then trigger future math anxieties. Math classrooms are especially prone to traumatizing events because of the emphasis on speed and accuracy, public individual performances, student labeling, one-shot tests, and a long history of cultural negativity. Most students who suffer from math anxiety can point to a particular traumatic event where math no longer made sense or became too painful to learn. For example, Kyndall can recall people telling him that their math anxieties started when they couldn't successfully recall all their math facts during timed tests in elementary school. Their feelings of failure and shame stayed with them into adulthood. Imagine what it must feel like to be labeled a failure in math as early as third grade. For this reason, it is important for teachers to peel back the layers to look beyond grades on a paper to the story and events that led up to those grades. We recommend a math autobiography, which we will describe in more detail later in this chapter, as a good way to help learn your students' stories.

IMPACT OF NOT UNDERSTANDING YOUR STUDENTS

Deficit thinking

One problem that results from not understanding students well is that teachers tend to see marginalized students only in terms of their deficits and not their strengths. Deficit thinking is a natural outgrowth of negative stereotypes. Too often, when these students struggle academically, negative stereotypes are reinforced in their

---

6 Ibid.

teachers' minds, resulting in lowered expectations and blame toward students for their own failure, perhaps because they couldn't complete their homework or the teacher believes they are simply lazy. In addition, teachers may inaccurately assume that students cannot learn a new skill because they have not mastered the necessary prerequisites.

These biases partly result from teachers' unwillingness to acknowledge the racial and ethnic identities of their students or to see students as individuals. Teachers who do this do not realize the powerful motivation that cultural contexts can provide for students to learn. The fear that comes from stereotyping students can cut teachers off from a wealth of cultural knowledge that could later be used as a foundation to build new knowledge. This is especially important when teaching math concepts that can be particularly abstract.

For example, the diagrams below show the same concepts represented in a variety of ways. Effective teachers help students make connections between these representations to deepen their understanding of the math topic. Because of the way that abstract representations are privileged over visual and contextual representations in traditional math classes, students often are satisfied with only knowing math concepts in one way. To help students understand the importance of multiple representations, teachers can help students recognize how different representations reveal different aspects of the same thing, just like ice, water, and steam all display different aspects of H_2O. The diagrams below show how a student's favorite song can be represented in four different ways, just like a linear function can be represented in different ways.

CD	Digital Download	Video	Concert

Four Representations of a Song

Verbal	Algebraic	Numerical	Graphical
The output is the opposite of the input increased by two.	$y = -x + 2$	x y -1 3 0 2 1 1 2 0	

Four Representations of a Linear Function

Missed opportunities to build relationships

Pedagogical theorist and teacher educator Gloria Ladson-Billings advocates for the use of culturally relevant teaching as a strategy for teachers to understand their students. She distinguishes between student–teacher relationships that are culturally relevant and those that are assimilationist.

Assimilationist teaching is "a teaching style that operates without regard to the student's particular cultural characteristics." These kinds of student–teacher relationships are fixed and hierarchical. They foster competitive achievement, result in connections with a few select students, and lead to hyperindividualism and isolation. Assimilationist teachers expect students to conform to their perception of what it means to be a good student, which is often informed by White, Eurocentric norms, meaning non-White students feel like they have to abandon their own culture in order to become successful in school.[7]

Culturally relevant relationships are, by contrast, fluid, humane, and equitable. In culturally relevant classrooms, teachers and students co-construct academic and behavioral norms and hold each other accountable for maintaining those norms. Culturally relevant teachers encourage connections with all students, emphasize collaboration, and establish communities of learners. Students work

---

7   Gloria Ladson-Billings, *The Dreamkeepers: Successful Teachers of African-American Children* (San Francisco: Jossey-Bass, 1994), 22.

on real-world activities and projects that foster interdependence and allow students to use their community-based knowledge to solve problems.

In their book, *Fires in the Middle School Bathroom*, Kathleen Cushman and Laura Rogers demonstrate the importance of building positive relationships with students. Middle school students shared with the authors that, when they feel teachers don't care what they think, they end up hating them. A common response of adolescents to indifferent teachers is to reject connections and take a more adversarial stance.[8]

Oftentimes, teachers don't understand the connection between their relationship with students and their performance. Some teachers take the stand that their job is to teach and not be a student's "friend." Teachers need to find ways to let students know they care about them. This can be done by having verbal check-ins, journal writes, math autobiographies, or entry and exit tickets. When students see a teacher making an effort to understand them as people, the students are more likely to feel that the teacher cares about them.

Lack of effort and low achievement

Having limited knowledge of our students can impact achievement in unintended ways. When teachers don't understand their students well, culturally based misunderstandings can lead to feelings of disrespect, which can undermine positive student–teacher relationships.[9]

Examples of culturally based misunderstandings include perceptions of what kind of behavior is considered aggressive and students and teachers not understanding each other's sense of humor.

---

8 Kathleen Cushman and Laura Rogers, *Fires in the Middle School Bathroom: Advice for Teachers from Middle Schoolers* (New York: New Press, 2008).

9 Vicki Nishioka, "Building Connections with Students from Diverse Cultural Backgrounds through Perspective-Taking," Institute of Education Sciences, May 11, 2018, https://ies.ed.gov/ncee/edlabs/regions/northwest/blog/building-connections .asp.

Sometimes, what a teacher perceives as student laziness or not caring is really a sense of hopelessness and despair.

A study out of Chicago found that one of the characteristics that distinguished the most successful schools was "strong social relationships among students and adults in and out of school."[10] The academic gains of schools that lacked strong social relationships were 47 percent lower than those of schools with strong social relationships. When students perceive that their teachers do not understand them, they disengage from the academic work of the class.

COMING TO UNDERSTAND YOUR STUDENTS

Pam once had a student named Myra. On one occasion, because of her misbehavior in class, Pam snapped at her, and after that, Myra refused to answer questions, participate in class, or complete her assignments. Myra would walk into class, sit in her assigned seat, and do very little else. This behavior continued for weeks, until Pam decided to try something she had recently learned at a conference. During a class change, she stood at the doorway and shook the hand of every student as they entered the room. When Myra arrived, Pam stretched out her hand. Myra stopped, looked at her, and limply held out her hand so Pam could shake it. Afterward, she sat down in her seat, quietly, as usual. However, during the class period her frosty reception slowly melted, and before the end of the period, she was asking and answering questions, fully engaged in the math lesson.

Before that handshake, Pam had only seen Myra in terms of her behavior, which she viewed as a challenge to her authority. Although we might be saddened by a student's lack of engagement, it may not dawn on us to think about what our responses to their behavior communicate about our care, or lack thereof. When a student makes the decision not to learn from you, something as simple as a handshake

---

10 Lisa Delpit,"*Multiplication Is for White People": Raising Expectations for Other People's Children* (New York: New Press, 2012).

can help you connect (or reconnect) on a human level, putting you on a path to being able to learn mathematics together.

Although connecting with students may be difficult, it is important for teachers to always maintain a posture of openness to doing things that can improve their relationships with students. It is important to note that Pam continually made attempts to connect with Myra, even when Myra did not immediately reciprocate. If Pam had stubbornly waited for Myra to "come to her senses," the outcome would probably have been Myra's failure of the class. Because so many students depend on us for school success, it is imperative that we not hold grudges and continue to seek to connect (or reconnect) with all our students, even those whose behavior may be challenging.

When Pam was in college, one of her professors told her that teaching and learning is a love relationship between a teacher and a child. She had never thought about it that way, but she believed it. Just as with people we love, these relationships are often complicated. How do we communicate that love in ways students accept and appreciate? How do we steer clear of behaviors that dominate and/or depreciate their value? The fact that we teach mathematics can make this type of relationship so much more difficult because of students' difficult history and love-hate relationship with the subject.

Some of the reasons people give for loving mathematics are that it helps them with money, it makes them look and feel smart when they are good at it, and it challenges them in a good way. Others say they hate mathematics because it's hard and confusing and it makes them look and feel dumb when they are not good at it.

Just as in any relationship, students weigh the pros and cons to decide if this is a relationship worth investing in. Many of our students decide the cons outweigh the pros and choose not to invest their energy in learning mathematics. That's where we come in as the teacher. We need to ask our students to separate their relationship with us from their relationship with mathematics, which is really hard to do since we ask them to engage in math every day! Students need to know that we care about them apart from their relationship with mathematics. The goal is for them to be able to relate to us positively, even when their relationship with math may not be so positive.

As teachers, we also need to separate that relationship in our own minds, especially when we find ourselves reacting emotionally to students' lack of effort, knowledge, or care about the mathematics we are trying to teach them. Can we really separate these relationships? Because teaching is so deeply personal, we may still find ourselves taking so much of what we do with our students personally—but we must try. Understanding our students well means that we know their math histories (both successes and failures), and we understand how these experiences impact the ways they currently experience mathematics.

Math story

So how do we do this? We ask them to share their math story. When our students are opening up about their histories with mathematics, they need to know that even their teachers' relationships with math may not have always been positive—no relationship is always positive. This means we need to share our stories as well. We also need to let them know that they are still writing their math stories and that it is up to them to decide what they want that story to be. We are writing that story together; all of us are a part of each other's story.

We help our students begin to write their stories with the following prompts:

- My first memories of math were ...
- I was good (or wasn't good) at math until ...
- Now math is ...

Morgan's Story

Math was always easy for me in elementary and middle school. I loved getting called on to answer a math problem, and I always challenged my mom to multiplication. I loved math so much that I started teaching my cousin how to multiply. I knew all of my multiplication problems. I was so good at multiplication that my teacher decided to make me go against the whole class. I remember that was the first time I realized that I was really good at math. I'm not going to lie—the very first time I saw a math problem, I said to myself, "I'm not going to like this," but I turned out to be wrong.

What made math more exciting for me was my third-grade teacher. She always let me come to her class to study and practice my homework, and every time I was stuck, she helped me through. She was like a mom in school. All the students loved her. I loved going to her class because she always had math games. I remember this one game where everyone sat in a circle, and she had a bag of marbles, and she would pass it around so everyone could guess how many marbles were in the bag. You couldn't say your number out loud; you had to write it down and put your number in a jar. Whoever was closest would get to teach the other students multiplication. Every time I played, I got closest to the answer. I remember I taught the whole class multiplication for a whole week. That was one of my favorite math experiences.

The time I realized I started disliking math was in eighth grade. The teacher gave the class a problem, and that was the first time I saw letters in a math problem. I went to my teacher and told her she put a letter in the problem, and she said, "I know. This is a new way for math." So I went to attempt the problem, but somehow I could never get it right. I was so mad that everyone else was getting the problem right and I wasn't that I walked out of class and went to Mr. Neal's room. I sat in his class until it was time to go home. When I got home, I studied that problem all night, and I still didn't get it. So I gave up, and ever since then I stopped liking math.

By reading students' math stories, we learn things about them that their schoolwork can't tell us. We can identify traumatizing math experiences and when math stopped making sense to them. We can find places of pain, as well as joy and triumphs. Reading their stories again at the end of the year will help you understand the impact you've had on your students' confidence in their math abilities, as well as show you areas where you need to improve. Having students tell their math stories will help you see them as human beings with hopes, fears, and aspirations, which often gets lost in a test-driven culture.

Journaling

Beyond students telling their math stories, journaling, in general, can be a useful tool for understanding your students better. Journals are often used in language arts classrooms to get students to write about their understanding of the content, but they are becoming more common in the mathematics classroom as a place for students to take notes, work problems, and explain their mathematical thinking. Journals are also a communication tool that can give teachers valuable insight so they can provide guidance and feedback to their students. Teachers can have students complete journal prompts daily or weekly. Each time a student makes a journal entry, a teacher should respond, whether it is regarding the student's solution to a mathematics task or their opinion about a personal issue. This interaction can help to build a positive teacher–student relationship.

When presented with the idea of using journals in the math classroom, many teachers initially react by saying they don't have the time to read journals and give feedback. It does take time to read through an entire classroom's journals, or multiple classrooms' journals, every day. One option would be to divide the class into groups and read one group's journals each day. Secondary teachers can choose one period a day to read.

Another option is to allow students to read and give feedback to each other. Pam used online journals, which were easier to read. The journal entries can be placed in a discussion group for students to read, provide feedback, and vote for the best entry. The author of the winning journal entry can be rewarded with points, a homework pass, or some other privilege.

We've learned from reading our students' math stories that many aren't good in math because, even though they know how important it is, they aren't motivated to put in the effort needed to learn it. To be honest, you might be frequently frustrated that your efforts to reason with students about the importance of hard work for their future often go unheard. However, it may be encouraging to know that, according to research by psychologist David DeSteno, willpower and grit are not the best routes to success. Instead, the social emotions of gratitude, compassion, and pride are key to motivating people to develop the habits of self-control and delayed gratification that are so critical for future success.[11] Therefore, we use writing prompts that include these factors. We also make sure to incorporate these ideas into the feedback we give to students by letting them know what they did correctly and providing guidance for how to correct mistakes without doing the work for them. In our classrooms, we have used the following prompts:

- What are you grateful for in this math class?
- How did you help somebody in class today?
- What did you do that made you proud? Why did it make you proud?

Our students have expressed gratitude for the safety of their learning environment and the motivation and perseverance they've gained through learning about growth mindset, compassion to help their classmates when they need it, and pride in acing an assignment with material they don't normally excel at. You may be surprised at just how well students respond to this prompt!

---

11 David DeSteno, "Three Emotions That Can Help You Succeed at Your Goals," *Greater Good Magazine,* January 12, 2018, https://greatergood.berkeley.edu/article/item /three_emotions_that_can_help_you_succeed_at_your_goals.

Team-building activities

An additional way to understand your students well is to engage them in team-building activities. Team-building activities help students get to know the teacher and each other better, which sets the stage for the kind of discourse that is recommended for mathematics classes in many state and national mathematics standards.

There are many ways to develop a social contract with a class of students. The process includes allowing all students to brainstorm how they should treat others and how they want to be treated by others. After brainstorming, all students are given the opportunity to offer their ideas to the social contract. Ideas are recorded on chart paper, and the class refines the list by consensus. When an agreement is reached, everyone signs the contract, including the teacher, and the social contract is then placed prominently in the classroom.

Everyone, each student and the teacher, has the right to point out when the social contract has been violated. An example of a norm is "No put-downs" or "Students should not make negative statements about one another." A process for pointing out violations must be included as part of the contract. If one student were to put another student down, students can say a code word, like *Cooper* to signal to the offender in a gentle reaffirming way that the social contract has been violated. The consequence would be for the offending student to apologize to the student who was offended. This offers an opportunity to reinforce the social contract and hold everyone accountable to classroom norms.[12]

Communication styles

One of the effective teaching practices outlined in NCTM's *Principles to Actions* is facilitating meaningful mathematical discourse. This

---

12 "Social Contracts: A Proactive Intervention for the Classroom," University of Minnesota, http://ceed.umn.edu/wp-content/uploads/2017/05/Social-Contracts.pdf; "Classroom Contract," The Teacher Toolkit, https://www.theteachertoolkit.com/index. php/tool/classroom-contract.

allows students to build a shared understanding of mathematical ideas by analyzing and comparing student approaches to arguments.[13]

If a teacher is going to engage their students in discourse, it is important for them to understand their students' communication styles so they can plan their instruction accordingly, assign group roles appropriately, and create optimal learning spaces for all students. Teachers need to ascribe value to all communication styles, not just those favored by traditional schooling practice.

Understanding student communication styles also helps to create norms for collaboration. When a student understands their own communication style, it helps them to be more metacognitive. When students understand the communication styles of their classmates, they are better able to have positive interactions in group settings.

An activity that helps teachers and students identify their own communication styles and recognize the communication styles of others is Hawk, Rabbit, Tiger, Turtle. In this activity, a poster with the name of one of these four animals is placed in each corner of the room, and students are asked to identify the animal that best matches their own individual style of communication. Then, with others who made the same choice, they discuss why they picked that animal, reflect on the different communication styles represented by each animal, and consider how they can most effectively communicate. Appendix E contains detailed information about this activity.

Another strategy for helping teachers and students learn more about each other is the Find Someone Who activity previously mentioned in chapter 1 (see p. 32). In this version of the activity, the teacher and students learn information about each other they may not otherwise have found out. Instead of working math problems, students are given a bingo-like game board with different descriptions of types of people in each box. Their task is to get as many signatures as possible that fit the descriptions—for example, find

13 National Council of Teachers of Mathematics, *Principles to Actions: Ensuring Mathematical Success for All* (Reston, VA: NCTM, 2014).

someone who was born the same month as you; find someone who has lived in a different city; find someone who has a grandparent living with them; find someone who speaks more than one language. Teachers can create descriptions that meet the unique characteristics of their classes.

Student interest survey: What does success look like?

One year Pam decided to do something to collect more than just general student information about her students. Pam wanted to know more about their expectations from a math class, so she asked her high school students to complete an online survey with the following questions:

- What do you think are the qualities that make a good teacher?
- What are you passionate about?
- What are your strengths?
- What is one thing you would like me to know about you?

Pam learned that most of her students wanted a teacher who was understanding and patient. While Pam tended to value an efficient use of class time and deep understanding of the content, she realized that she had to make sure her focus on these things didn't cause her to lose patience or be too busy to listen and see things from her students' perspectives. She also discovered that she could use her students' passion for technology, music, sports, cosmetology, astronomy, family, and art as contexts for math concepts they would be learning throughout the year. One thing that really struck her was how many of her students could not identify any strengths at all. This information made her more committed to using the strategy of assigning competence to her students during class. Some of the most valuable information gleaned was from answers to the question, "What is one thing you want me to know about you?" Pam was pleasantly surprised at how self-aware many of her students were.

Students sharing about their sense of humor, anger problems, laziness, and/or difficulty with math at the beginning of the semester meant Pam could use this information to better meet their needs. She did not have to rely on stereotypes about her students, who were all African American. She had concrete information about her students to guide the myriad instructional decisions she had to make throughout the course of the semester. Because she collected this information online, she was able to easily revisit it when she needed to figure out how to motivate a struggling student or how to celebrate growth/achievement.

— QUESTIONS TO CONSIDER —

1. What attitudes and beliefs do you have that inhibit your ability to get to know your students more broadly?
2. How can you create learning contexts for your students that will help them engage more meaningfully with the mathematics they need to learn?

— CALL TO ACTION —

1. List the two ideas you learned from this chapter that are most relevant to your practice.
2. Complete the action plan on the following page for each idea.

Idea 1:	
Vision for your students if you implement this idea in your classroom, school, or district	
Action step	
Deadline for action step	
Person you will ask to hold you accountable for completing this action step	

Idea 2:	
Vision for your students if you implement this idea in your classroom, school, or district	
Action step	
Deadline for action step	
Person you will ask to hold you accountable for completing this action step	

CHAPTER FOUR

USE CULTURALLY RELEVANT CURRICULA

As I contemplated how to approach my Advanced Mathematical Decision Making class, I thought, "What am I going to do with Jasmine?" Like the majority of her classmates, Jasmine was failing a senior-level math class that she needed to graduate from high school. What made Jasmine different was that she had openly expressed her hostility toward me on several occasions and had been referred to the administration for disciplinary action as a result. Jasmine very seldom completed classwork, refused to answer questions when she was called on in class, refused to collaborate with her classmates, and would often try to sleep in class. Despite my efforts to engage Jasmine in math lessons, she made it very clear that she was not interested in doing anything I required. I was spending a lot of emotional energy and class time getting her to cooperate, and this investment didn't seem to be paying off.

I could sense that many of my students struggled to see the connection between the math they were learning and their personal lives. Ultimately, I considered the Georgia Milestones project that I'd previously developed for my ninth-grade students to keep them focused during the last few weeks of school. The Georgia Milestones Assessment System was a statewide summative assessment program in the areas of math, English language arts, science, and social studies. In elementary and middle school, the assessments were used to determine student promotion and retention. In high school, assessment scores counted as 20 percent of the students' final grade. Even though the results of state tests were discussed ad nauseum in data team meetings, faculty meetings, and parent meetings, the students taking these tests were rarely a part of these conversations. However, because of the data analysis they would do for this project, it might potentially enable them to meaningfully contribute to these conversations. But I wondered if this project would be interesting enough to engage my seniors, especially Jasmine. Would they put forth the effort to complete the work or would they fail to turn in assignments like they'd done on many previous occasions? There was only one way to find out, so I assigned my seniors the project and held my breath.

For the project, students were asked to go to various state websites to determine the percentage of Black students at the twenty-three high schools in our school district and the most current passing rates for the state's Coordinate Algebra and Analytic Geometry End-of-Course Assessments. After organizing this information in an Excel spreadsheet, they created a scatterplot of the data and a regression equation and used that information to answer the following questions:

1. What type of correlation do you notice? Strong or weak; positive or negative? Explain.

2. Which schools seem to be significantly above your trend line? Which schools seem to be significantly below your trend line? What do you think was different about these schools that caused them to be significantly above or below the trend line?

3. Use your regression equation to predict our school's passing rate for Coordinate Algebra or Analytic Geometry Milestones. How close was the actual passing rate to the predicted rate? Was it higher or lower? Why?

4. Write a paragraph (at least five sentences) summarizing your thoughts about this data. Be sure to include answers to the following questions:
   - What conclusions can you draw from your analysis of this data?
   - What questions does this data raise for you?
   - What recommendations would you make to the incoming freshman for improving the passing rates for the Georgia Milestones next year?
   - What recommendations would you make to the math teachers?
   - What recommendations would you make to the administrative team?

Once my students got past the technical requirements of the assignment, such as locating needed files, figuring out how to access the data, computing percentages when given only the numbers of the subgroups, and figuring out how to graph and/or create a trend line in Excel, they were actually quite engaged with the project. I spoke to several of my students about how the project impacted them. One shared that he liked how I encouraged them to find the percentages then make the scatterplots themselves, rather than merely asking them how they felt about the test scores. When I asked them how they felt about the data, they all agreed that it was pretty awful and left them feeling down. Then when I asked for their thoughts on why I had them do the assignment, they said that they knew it wasn't done to make them feel bad but to show them that they could make a change and that school is not all fun and games.

The impact this project had on Jasmine was even more remarkable. She seemed to be engaged in a way I had never seen from her before. Immediately, she began to ask me questions about the project, and she even asked if she could work with a partner. When I helped her realize her calculations were incorrect, rather than submit the project with errors, she willingly chose to redo them. On the last day of the project, she stayed after school to put on the finishing touches. Not only did I see a positive *change in her involvement with the math lesson, I also noticed that her hostility toward me had vanished. Instead, she'd become kind, pleasant, and warm with both me and her classmates. Because of this marked difference, I chose to speak to her privately about how this project impacted her. She shared with me that she had found the project both fun and interesting. For her, it was not just about getting the grade. She really wanted to find out the information.*

Reflecting on her willing participation in this project, I began to realize that it had been an effective way for her to channel her energies, anger, and desire to resist a system that she perceived as unfair. I later recognized that her behavior that undermined the learning environment and rejected my authority was her attempt to challenge an education system that she felt did not adequately serve her needs or the needs of her African American peers. I began to understand the importance of students being able to see themselves reflected in the materials and resources used in the mathematics classroom.

— Pam

USE CULTURALLY RELEVANT CURRICULA

Being a culturally relevant teacher means using instructional materials in ways that help students see themselves as doers of mathematics and help them overcome the negative stereotypes and messages regarding who is—and who isn't—mathematically smart.

Culturally relevant pedagogy "empowers students intellectually, socially, emotionally, and politically by using cultural referents to impart knowledge, skills, and attitudes." In 1994, Gloria Ladson-Billings, professor in the Department of Curriculum and Instruction at the University of Wisconsin–Madison, published her groundbreaking book, *The Dreamkeepers: Successful Teachers of African*

American Children.[1] In this book, she described the three pillars of culturally relevant pedagogy as follows: (1) academic achievement, (2) cultural competence, and (3) critical consciousness. This work was groundbreaking because of its departure from the deficit models that were so prevalent at the time as explanations for the underachievement of students who were Black, Hispanic, and from other marginalized groups.

Initially, social Darwinism justified the notion of superiority of Anglo-Saxons over other ethnic groups through its survival-of-the-fittest ideology.[2] Later these ideas of biological and racial superiority were replaced with ideas of cultural superiority. Ethnicity theory promoted the idea of the model minority that was able to overcome poverty, prejudice, and hardships through assimilation and hard work. The insinuation is that Blacks, Hispanics, and other groups that remain on the bottom of society are there because of cultural deficiencies. Ethnicity theory applied to education has resulted in the cultural, socioeconomic, and environmental factors of students from diverse backgrounds being used to explain school failure. The cultural deprivation paradigm assumes that Black, Hispanic, and poor children, "because of cultural, biological, environmental, and social differences, lack the adaptations and knowledge necessary for school achievement."[3] Culturally relevant pedagogy challenges the notion that ethnic and socioeconomic minorities must put aside their own cultural values and embrace White, middle-class values to be successful in school.

We believe that culturally relevant teachers use curriculum materials to help expand students' visions of themselves as doers and creators of mathematics. We often ask ourselves, "Are my students

---

1 Gloria Ladson-Billings, *The Dreamkeepers: Successful Teachers of African American Children* (San Francisco: Jossey-Bass, 1994), 17–18.

2 Richard Hofstadter, *Social Darwinism in American Thought* (Boston: Beacon Press, 1955).

3 Jacqueline Jordan Irvine, *Black Students and School Failure: Policies, Practices, and Prescriptions* (Westport, CT: Greenwood Press, 1990).

able to engage in mathematical activities that reflect their interests, personalities, and cultural identities?"

As Rudine Sims Bishop, professor emerita of education at The Ohio State University, said, curricula should act as mirrors, windows, and sliding glass doors.[4] Students need curricula in which they can see reflections of themselves. Curricula can also be windows that students look through to see other worlds and how they either match up or don't to their own. But the sliding glass door allows students to enter that world as well. Multicultural curriculum materials, therefore, are beneficial not only for students who have been underrepresented or marginalized, but also for students from the dominant group.

Culturally relevant teachers understand that the mathematical experiences of students in their classes will either reinforce or challenge negative stereotypes and messages regarding who is mathematically smart. Since students from marginalized groups are less likely to see themselves as mathematicians, asking them to identify themselves as mathematicians during classroom activities is not necessarily an effective approach. To get them interested in actual math tasks, it is better to use action-oriented language that emphasizes the value of doing the task. For example, in a recent study some children were told they would be "doing science," while others were told that they would "be a scientist." Girls in the study who were asked to "do science" persisted longer in the task than the girls who were asked to "be scientists." Boys younger than five responded more favorably to action-oriented language, while older boys showed greater persistence when identity-oriented language was used.[5] This particular finding is thought to be the result of older boys being able to more easily identify with the stereotype of scientists being White and male.

---

4 Rudine Sims Bishop, "Mirrors, Windows, and Sliding Glass Doors," *Collected Perspectives: Choosing and Using Books for the Classroom* 6, no. 3 (Summer 1990): ix–xi.

5 Marjorie Rhodes et al., "Subtle Linguistic Cues Increase Girls' Engagement in Science," *Psychological Science* 30, no. 3 (2019): 455–66.

This study did not disaggregate the data by race. Because scientists share the same image problem as mathematicians, the findings from this study suggest that using identity-oriented language, such as "being a mathematician or scientist," can undermine the persistence of students who reject these identities due to cultural stereotypes.

WHY USING CULTURALLY RELEVANT CURRICULA IS AN EQUITY ISSUE

Where am I in this picture? is the question we ask when viewing a group photo. Likewise, students ask themselves the same question in mathematics classrooms. For many students, negative stereotypes and messages tell them that they do not belong in the picture of successful mathematicians. They hear messages like, "I can't do math," "Math is boring," and "Math has nothing to do with real life!"

The media often portray people who excel in mathematics as socially inept nerds who are White or Asian and rarely as people from marginalized groups. For example, according to Urban Dictionary, a crowdsourced online dictionary for slang words and phrases, a "math boy" is a "doer of math, unable to integrate with society—only functions of *x*."[6] For many students, being a "doer of math" conjures up images of old White men with crazy-looking hair, drab clothing, and thick-rimmed glasses. Most teenagers, however, value being cool, popular, and socially adept. While students may frequently see people in their communities and people of color in general celebrated for being good in sports or the performing arts, the role that mathematics plays in the success of many of their role models tends to be less obvious. Stereotypical images of mathematicians don't represent who these teenagers are now or who they desire to become in the future. This affects not only students of color, but also girls of all races. Because they may feel math achievement is

---

6 Retrieved from Urban Dictionary, http://www.urbandictionary.com/define.php?term=
math%20boy.

only for those few weird people who spend all of their time in books and have no social skills, many students choose not to embrace the hard work of learning math.

Unfortunately, this type of stereotypical thinking often limits students' views of themselves and their abilities to be successful in careers that require strong backgrounds in mathematics. The problem with stereotypes is not that they are untrue. Most math majors can probably recall having math professors who fit their mental image of the generic math nerd. The problem with stereotypes is that they are incomplete, with those not fitting the image feeling left out, devalued, and/or that they are the exception.[7]

In order to make math achievement more equitable, teachers must broaden students' images of successful math achievers to include people with whom they can identify. Culturally relevant teachers ask themselves, "Are people who look like my students positively portrayed in the materials I use?"

WHAT HAPPENS WHEN WE DON'T USE CULTURALLY RELEVANT CURRICULA

When teachers fail to use culturally relevant curricula, students who don't identify with the stereotypical image of those who are smart at mathematics may reject mathematics altogether. Not only is this rejection problematic for their future opportunities, it can also have more immediate ramifications in the math classroom. When students are continually asked to participate in mathematical activities they have rejected, they may manifest this rejection in the form of anger, defiance, and/or withdrawal.

As described in the narrative that started this chapter, Jasmine exhibited all three of these responses in Pam's class. She would often

---

7 Chimamanda Ngozi Adichie, "The Danger of a Single Story," TED video, 18:34, July 24, 2009, https://www.ted.com/talks/chimamanda_ngozi_adichie_the_danger_of_a _single_story/transcript?language=en#t-15566.

disrupt class by engaging in off-task conversations during class discussions. Attempts to redirect her were routinely met by rude remarks directed at the teacher, which often resulted in her removal from class. Even though she had rejected mathematics, Jasmine still wanted to be a part of the class. Upon her return to class after disciplinary action, she chose to put her head down on the desk, rather than risking getting put out of class again. When asked to sit up so she could engage in the assignment, Jasmine would respond in anger, saying things like, "You are always picking on me" or "I hate this class!" When asked questions in class, she would defiantly ignore them and refuse to respond.

No classroom management techniques would address the root cause of Jasmine's anger, defiance, and withdrawal in Pam's math class. What Pam saw as a classroom management issue was really an identity and representation issue. Jasmine was asked to engage in activities that did not align with her identity on a daily basis. Teachers who fail to use culturally relevant curricula run the risk of alienating students who do not see themselves represented in the curriculum, which can ultimately lead to students' rejection of anything related to mathematics.

Another consequence of teachers failing to use culturally relevant curricula is that students develop stereotypical ideas about who is mathematically smart along racial, ethnic, and socioeconomic lines. These stereotypical ideas can show up in the form of microaggressions in the classroom.

According to researcher Derald Wing Sue, professor of psychology at Teachers College, Columbia University, microaggressions are the "brief and everyday slights, insults, indignities and denigrating messages sent to people of color by well-intentioned White people who are unaware of the hidden messages being communicated."[8] Microaggressions that reinforce stereotypical ideas about who is mathematically smart can be especially damaging for students from marginalized groups. Statements like "You are so articulate" and "You are really smart" may have good intentions behind them but can communicate the hidden message that the person being addressed is the exception because most people who belong to that group aren't articulate or smart. Below are some ways that microaggressions may show up in a math classroom.

Statement	Hidden Message
To the Black male athlete in an honors math class: "We know you won't have time to study because you have a game tonight."	Based on stereotypes, you can't be good at sports AND academics.
To the female student who takes longer to respond to a classmate's question: "Since you don't know the answer, I'll ask someone else."	If you don't answer quickly, you are not as smart as the people in the class who do.
To the Black male student in the class: "Can you rap this math formula for us?"	As a Black person, your contribution is limited to entertainment, not academics.
To the new non-White student upon entering the honors math class: "Are you sure you are in the right class?'	Whiteness is the norm for being in honors math classes. Therefore, you must not belong.

---

8   Derald Wing Sue, "Racial Microaggressions in Everyday Life: Is Subtle Bias Harmless?" *Psychology Today,* October 5, 2010, https://www.psychologytoday.com /us/blog/microaggressions-in-everyday-life/201010/racial-microaggressions -in-everyday-life.

Fusion TV, a Univision network with programming geared toward Hispanic Americans, has posted a video that compares microaggressions to mosquito bites.[9] For people who rarely experience them, they may seem trivial and a minor annoyance. Each mosquito bite represents a microaggression experienced by a person of color on a regular basis. The cumulative effect of microaggressions is similar to the cumulative effect of multiple mosquito bites over time. Multiple mosquito bites can run the range of slightly annoying, to pain, to disease or even death. Likewise, the cumulative impact of microaggressions can result in stress, anxiety, and limited educational or employment opportunities, which can ultimately lead to homelessness and/or incarceration. Microaggressions left unchecked can have long-term negative consequences on the mental and academic well-being of students of color.

Traditional classroom practices often reinforce stereotypical views of mathematical smartness. In traditional classrooms, students watch the teacher or competent classmates work math problems while they passively copy the procedures in a notebook. Academic success depends on their ability to replicate these procedures on similar problems on future class assignments, homework, quizzes, and tests. Very seldom does it occur to most students that they can figure out ways of solving problems that they have never seen before. Doing mathematics is left to teachers or those really "smart" people who seem to have that "math gene."

In his 2016 TEDx Talk, Dan Finkel, founder of Math for Love, a Seattle-based organization devoted to transforming how math is taught and learned said, "We can't afford to misuse math by creating passive rule followers."[10] We find his use of the word *misuse* very appropriate, especially when applied to students of color. Passivity

9 Fusion Comedy, "How Microaggressions Are Like Mosquito Bites," Fusion TV video, 1:57, October 5, 2016, https://fusion.tv/video/354460/how-microaggressions-are-like-mosquito-bites/.

10 Dan Finkel, "Five Principles of Extraordinary Math Teaching," TED video, 14:42, February 17, 2016, https://www.youtube.com/watch?v=ytVneQUA5-c&feature=youtu.be.

promotes compliance rather than engagement. Compliance reinforces the status quo and perpetuates the achievement gap. Students with instructional gaps continue to fall further behind each year because they cannot remember the rules or how to regurgitate the procedures given to them by their teachers. As the gaps grow, their self-confidence and sense of efficacy drop.

On the other hand, effective teachers focus on engagement, not compliance. In order for classrooms to be more equitable, teachers must be explicit about what it means to be a doer of mathematics. The characteristics of student thinking while doing mathematical tasks include the following:

- Thinking in a complex and nonalgorithmic manner
- Exploring and understanding the nature of mathematical concepts, processes, or relationships
- Demanding self-monitoring or self-regulation of one's own cognitive processes
- Accessing relevant knowledge and experiences and making appropriate use of them in working through the task
- Analyzing tasks and actively examining task constraints that may limit possible solution strategies and solutions
- Applying considerable cognitive effort and involving some level of anxiety for the student due to the unpredictable nature of the solution process[11]

Our experiences as classroom teachers, coaches, and support providers for pre-service and in-service teachers have given us the opportunity to identify a number of experiences that reinforce negative stereotypes for students as doers of mathematics, such as the following:

- Failing math year after year
- Missing out on rewards or accolades because achievement is always below grade level

---

11 Mary Kay Stein et al., *Implementing Standards-Based Mathematics Instruction: A Casebook for Professional Development* (New York: Teachers College Press, 2009).

- Receiving feedback only about weaknesses, never strengths
- Avoiding wrong answers at all costs
- Feeling invisible in class because only the "smart" people get called on
- Seeing only a few students of color in honors, gifted, or accelerated classes
- Having creativity stifled when teachers recognize only one way of doing things
- Having a curriculum full of "naked" math problems devoid of meaningful contexts
- Giving only high achievers rigorous work that requires critical thinking
- Giving low-performing students a steady diet of low-level worksheets and drills on prerequisite skills that have not been mastered

BECOMING A CULTURALLY RELEVANT TEACHER

Just as we have learned that many things in our work as educators can reinforce negative stereotypes for math students, we likewise recognize experiences that challenge these stereotypes:

- Making good grades in math, despite poor past performance
- Celebrating growth, in addition to achievement
- Respecting mistakes and using them as bridges to future learning
- Providing multiple opportunities to show mastery
- Expecting all students to fully participate in class, with nobody allowed to "hide"
- Ensuring that students of color are proportionally represented in honors, gifted, or accelerated classes

- Allowing mastery of standards to be demonstrated in flexible and creative ways
- Engaging students in mathematical activities that reflect contexts that are meaningful to them and empower them to be doers of mathematics, rather than passive recipients of knowledge
- Providing the supports necessary for students to gain access to tasks that require higher-order thinking, regardless of previous history of poor performance

How can a teacher implement a culturally relevant curriculum in their mathematics classroom? We feel that to effectively use culturally relevant curricula, teachers need to attend to many different aspects of the learning environment, including learning about students' identities, using instructional resources that portray people of color positively, and cultivating active teaching strategies.

Honoring student identity

Using culturally relevant curricula requires that teachers acknowledge the racial and ethnic identities of their students. When teachers do take the time to get to know who their students are as people, they are better able to design mathematical tasks that are relevant to their lives. Many students of color are developing multiple identities at the same time, including gender, religious, academic, and racial identities.

Racial identity development can be defined as "the process of defining for oneself the personal significance and social meanings of belonging to a particular racial group." "An ethnic group is a socially defined group based on *cultural criteria*, such as language, customs, and a shared history."[12] Racial and ethnic identity formation can begin as early as junior high school. Schools can and do serve a

12 Beverly Tatum, *Why Are All the Black Kids Sitting Together in the Cafeteria? And Other Conversations about Race* (New York: Basic Books, 1997), 16.

powerful role in shaping students' academic identities. When African American students are able to connect with peers and supportive adults who encourage them to talk about personal issues that impact their academic achievement, a peer culture that supports academic performance develops.[13]

These same results can be replicated in mathematics classrooms that use culturally relevant curricula. If students are able to engage in mathematics tasks that are designed to address their experiences and community conditions, they can see that mathematics can be used to solve the real-world problems they face in their everyday lives. When students at an elementary school in New York City were having altercations in the hallways, teachers wanted to investigate the causes and develop a solution. After observing student behavior during class changes and on the way to or from lunch and recess, teachers began to wonder if overcrowding might be the issue. They then opted to engage their students in a real-life mathematics inquiry.

To investigate the overcrowding hypothesis, students used geometry to calculate the square footage of the hallway space, and they used proportional reasoning to calculate the student-per-square-foot ratios of their school and of the magnet school that shared the same building. When the students compared their ratio of student-per-square-foot to that of the magnet school, they found that their ratio was much higher. The students took their findings to the school board and requested the school population be decreased. The school board complied with the students' request, and the hallway altercations ceased. Because of their teachers' efforts to align their curricula to the lived experiences of their students, these students were able to see firsthand how mathematics can be used to effect change in their everyday lives.[14]

---

13 Ibid.

14 Erin E. Turner and Beatriz T. Font Strawhun, "With Math, It's Like You Have More Defense: Students Investigate Overcrowding at Their School," in *Rethinking Schools: Social Justice by the Numbers*, ed. Eric Gutstein and Bob Peterson (Milwaukee, WI: Rethinking Schools, 2013), 129–35.

To effectively implement culturally relevant curricula, teachers need to be cognizant of how instructional practices have been used to exclude students of color in mathematics. Math teachers of students from marginalized groups need to broaden their instructional practices beyond "teaching-to-the-test" and other narrow teaching strategies and provide students with a high-level, cognitively demanding mathematics curriculum. Their mathematics education should give African American students the ability to use math as a tool to improve their lives and collective conditions. There are many teachers who have used the history of discrimination against African Americans, critical media analysis, and community safety as topics to build relationships with their African American students and show them the importance of mathematics.

For example, one group of students explored the negative impact of the proliferation of liquor stores in their community. The students complained that they were often harassed by drunk people for money. After investigating, the students found that local legislation dictated the number of liquor stores allowed in any community. The goal of the project was the closure or relocation of thirteen stores in close proximity to their school. The students studied the local legislation related to zoning and liquor licenses and proposed alternative economic incentives that were based on mathematics to get the liquor stores to move to locations away from their school. Their actions resulted in the citation of two hundred liquor stores and the closure of two of the thirteen targeted stores for major violations.[15]

Instructional resources that favorably portray people of color

Few mathematics curricular materials include the contributions of people of color. This glaring omission has the potential to leave

---

15 William F. Tate, "Race, Retrenchment, and the Reform of School Mathematics," in *Rethinking Schools,* ed. Eric Gutstein and Bob Peterson (Milwaukee, WI: Rethinking Schools, 2017), 42–51.

students with the impression that only people of European descent have made significant additions to the field of mathematics.

The book *Beyond Banneker* chronicles the lives of the first African American man (Elbert Frank Cox) and woman (Euphemia Lofton Haynes) to receive a doctorate in mathematics. The author also interviewed thirty-five African Americans with doctorates in mathematics to find out who they were and what their paths to the profession were like. The work illustrates the impact that community and history can have in cultivating positive mathematical identities and explores the difficulties faced by African American mathematicians in terms of their perceived abilities. It shows how they created bonds with one another that have allowed them to collaborate and to contribute significantly to the field of mathematics.[16]

In that vein, we advocate for the incorporation of mathematics materials where people of color, women and girls, and other marginalized groups are favorably portrayed to provide examples that all students can aspire to. The website *Mathematicians of the African Diaspora* is a good place to start.[17]

Using active teaching strategies

A culturally relevant curriculum must actively engage students in learning mathematical concepts. Oftentimes, because of negative stereotypes about students of color, a teacher's fear of losing control will cause them to be reluctant to engage students in active learning strategies. (We will discuss this further in chapter 6.)

In education philosophy, the term *constructivism* describes the belief that learning is an active, constructive process where people connect prior learning to new information as part of the learning process. The philosophy of constructivism promotes the idea that

---

16 Erica N. Walker, *Beyond Banneker: Black Mathematicians and the Paths to Excellence* (Albany, NY: State University of New York Press, 2014).

17 Scott Williams, *Mathematicians of the African Diaspora*, last updated September 9, 2001, http://www.math.buffalo.edu/mad/00.INDEXmad.html.

learners actively create their own subjective representations of objective reality.

There are many examples of teaching strategies that can be classified as active learning. One strategy is collaborative learning, where students work together in small groups toward a common goal, often the completion of a task. This strategy can be enhanced by assigning group roles to make sure all students have the opportunity to engage meaningfully with the task at hand. Cooperative learning is an extension of collaborative learning in that it tends to the additional components of positive interdependence, individual accountability, equal interaction, and simultaneous interaction. Spencer Kagan offers a wealth of cooperative learning structures that address the social aspects of learning that can be applied to any content area.[18] Problem-based learning is another active learning strategy where relevant problems are used to provide context and motivation for learning. These active learning strategies have a positive impact on student learning.

Supporting student engagement in the Standards for Mathematical Practice

The Standards for Mathematical Practice are the behaviors of mathematically proficient students. Since they involve actions such as constructing viable arguments, critiquing the reasoning of others, and making use of structure, they are the pathway to building mathematical proficiency. Yet, many students of color are relegated to mindlessly following procedures taught by their teachers, and therefore do not have the opportunity to develop their problem-solving abilities. Students need to be confident in their problem-solving abilities in order to be mathematically proficient. They must be able to read a problem and understand what needs to be done to solve it, estimate

---

18 Spencer Kagan and Miguel Kagan, *Kagan Cooperative Learning* (San Clemente, CA: Kagan Publishing, 2009).

a solution, solve problems using multiple strategies, and evaluate problem solutions in context. Students of color, however, are rarely given opportunities to engage in high-level, cognitively demanding mathematics tasks.[19] Many times this is because teachers do not think low-performing students of color are capable of complex problem solving. This sets in place a vicious cycle in which students are never able to hone their problem-solving skills because teachers never provide them with opportunities to solve problems.

Making sense of a problem helps students see themselves as doers of mathematics. When students are able to read a problem, understand what it is asking, and compute the correct solution, they begin to trust in their own problem-solving abilities. It is important for teachers to provide opportunities for students to engage in authentic problem solving. We need to explicitly teach students problem-solving strategies, such as looking for patterns, making a table, or drawing a picture. Because students often have difficulty recognizing mathematical relationships embedded in word problems, literacy strategies, such as graphic organizers or the three-read protocol, help students understand the text. Pam uses the graphic organizer below to help students make sense of word problems. (See Appendix C for completed sample charts.)

Quantity	Units	Description	Expression

---

19 Robert Q. Berry III, "Mathematics Standards, Cultural Styles, and Learning Preferences: The Plight and the Promise of African American Students," *The Clearing House* 76, no. 5 (2003): 244–49.

1. Students start by recording all the numbers they see in the problem in the *Quantity* column.

2. They then go back to the problem to identify the units for each quantity and record them in the *Units* column.

3. Next, they write a brief description for each quantity in the *Description* column.

4. Then they put a question mark (?) in the quantity column for the unknown value(s) and add rows below if needed.

5. Next, they place an algebraic or numerical expression that represents each quantity in the *Expression* column.

6. If appropriate, they use the information from the table to help sketch a picture that shows the relationship between the quantities.

This graphic organizer benefits students in several ways:

- It provides a way for students to get started, which is half the battle! Because many students feel like they should be able to look at the problem and automatically know how to solve it, they feel dumb when they don't know how to work a problem after first reading it. Identifying the numbers and placing them in the chart is a task that just about every student is willing to do without fear of being wrong.

- The organization of the chart provides a sequence for how to gather, organize, and think about the information. After students identify the numbers, the headings of the adjacent columns remind them what to do next.

- The act of filling out the chart requires students to read and reread the text multiple times, which addresses the idea that students should know how to work the problem the first time they read it. While completing the chart, they most often aren't even thinking about the fact they have to read the passage several times. For them, this doesn't really feel like reading. They are just getting the information they need from the text to complete the chart.

- Because there is limited space in the *Description* column, students engage in higher-order thinking when they have to compact the words from the problem in a way that makes sense to them and can also fit into the chart.

- Adding the question mark to the chart helps them focus on what the problem is asking them to find, but only after they've had the chance to make sense of it first.

- Having all of the information in one place helps students see the relationships between quantities, making it easier to write equations that represent those relationships, which can later be solved to answer the problem.

Persevering in a task can help students to overcome negative stereotypes and messages about who is mathematically smart. When we give our students the skills needed to make sense of a problem and the strategies to come up with a solution, it is then up to them to put in the effort necessary to complete the task. By carefully scaffolding students' problem-solving experiences in ways that allow them to experience productive struggle, rather than frustration or defeat, we can help students learn that if they are willing to make this effort, they can be doers of mathematics.

In order to be mathematically proficient, students need to make sense of quantities and relationships. When solving problems involving quantities, students must decontextualize the quantities to perform computations and then contextualize the quantities to provide a solution to the problem. Students need to be able to create representations of the problem, taking into account the units and meanings of the quantities involved. When students are able to represent the relationships between quantities in a problem, they are better able to write a mathematical equation or inequality that represents that relationship and then solve it to answer the problem.

Students come to class with a variety of experiences that teachers can use to build their abstract and quantitative reasoning. It is important for teachers to recognize the out-of-school activities that students engage in that can support their mathematical understanding. One real-world example observed by researchers was the street children in Brazil who sell candy. Because of the fluctuating economy, the candy sellers are required to recalculate the price of their products to take into account the changing value of currency. When related to their work, these children are capable of carrying out complex problems involving percent of increase and decrease. However, when many of these same children were given similar problems at school disconnected from any context, they were unable to connect what they knew from their lives to school math.[20]

Model with Mathematics

When students model with mathematics, it means they have the ability to "apply the mathematics they know to solve problems arising in everyday life, society, and the workplace."[21] What this looks like is different depending on grade level, but when implemented well, it can help students see themselves as doers of mathematics. Teachers need to help students recognize patterns and then translate those patterns to mathematical expressions and equations. Students need to be able to represent their solutions using words, numbers, symbols, and pictures and be able to see the connections between these representations.

---

20 Geoffrey B. Saxe, "Candy Selling and Math Learning," *Educational Researcher* 17, no. 6 (1988): 14–21, doi:10.3102/0013189X017006014.

21 National Governors Association Center for Best Practices and Council of Chief State School Officers, *Common Core State Standards for Mathematics* (Washington, DC: NGA Center and CCSO, 2010).

Traditionally, students who have been labeled as "smart" are those who are highly proficient in performing procedural computations with speed and accuracy. Modeling with mathematics helps to redefine what being "smart" means. The smart student is the one who can solve problems accurately, in multiple ways, and can explain both the solutions to problems and how they know their answers are correct.

One way to help students learn to model with mathematics is embodied in the movement to teach mathematics for social justice, which means "to deepen students' understanding of society and to prepare them to be critical, active participants in a democracy."[22] Teachers can create lessons and projects that allow students to study the economic, social, and political conditions in their communities while learning important mathematical concepts at the same time. Eric Gutstein's "Driving While Black or Brown" is a good example of a social justice mathematics activity.[23] This activity explores the issue of racial profiling of people of color by law enforcement by examining traffic stop data from the state of California. The mathematical task is focused on probability concepts of randomness, experimental versus theoretical probability, the law of large numbers, and the design and conducting of simulations.

The first activity in the lesson is designed to help students determine the racial breakdown of the state of California and reinforce the concepts of experimental versus theoretical probability. Students will work together in groups with defined roles.

Each group of students is given a small bag with colored cubes to represent the racial breakdown of California. Use nineteen tan cubes (for Whites, 38%), nineteen red cubes (for Latinx, 38%), seven blue cubes (for Asians, 14%), three orange cubes (for African Americans,

---

22 Eric Gutstein and Bob Peterson, *Rethinking Mathematics: Teaching Social Justice by the Numbers* (Milwaukee, WI: Rethinking Schools, 2013), 1.

23 Eric Gutstein, "Driving While Black or Brown: A Mathematics Project about Racial Profiling," in *Rethinking Schools*, ed. Eric Gutstein and Bob Peterson (Milwaukee, WI: Rethinking Schools, 2017), 16–18.

6%), and two green cubes (for others, 4%) to approximate California's racial proportions. Do not tell the students the total number of cubes or how many of each color there are.

Students pick one cube from the bag without looking, record its color on a chart (tally marks work well), and replace the cube. They repeat this one hundred times, recording the totals on a chart after every ten picks. Each line of the chart is the cumulative total of picks. Tell students they are conducting an experiment (picking/replacing one hundred times), collecting data (recording each pick), and analyzing data (determining for their simulation how many cubes of each color are in the bag, the total number of cubes, and the California racial/ethnic percentages).

After all of the groups have finished the simulation activity, the reporter for each group shares their percentages for each racial group in California. If time permits, the class totals can be tallied. Next, each student responds to the following questions in their journals:

1. What do you think is in the bag? Why do you think this?
2. What happened as you picked more times, and what do you think would happen if you picked a thousand times?

The teacher calls on a few students to share their responses to the journal prompts with the class. After a few comments have been shared, the groups are instructed to empty the bag to determine the number of cubes of each color. The teacher reinforces the idea that the results obtained during the simulation represent the experimental probability of choosing a cube of a particular color. The percentages obtained from counting the cubes in the bag represent the theoretical probability of choosing a particular color.

The second activity in the lesson provides an opportunity for students to create their own simulation to investigate whether data from traffic stops by race represent a case of racial profiling. Students are given the following information to use to create a probability simulation:

Here are data from the *Los Angeles Times* newspaper analyzing traffic stop data from 2012 to 2017. Of 378,000
drivers stopped by the California Highway Patrol (CHP),
151,200 were Latinx. During the same period of time, the
Domestic Highway Enforcement Team (DHET), a team
of Los Angeles County sheriff's deputies who cruise the
5 Freeway stopping motorists in search of cars carrying
drugs, pulled over about 13,333 people. Of those stopped,
9,200 were Latinx.

Students will use what they learned in the first experiment to set
up their own simulation of this situation using the cubes and bags.
The students will pick and replace a cube one hundred times, record
the data, and calculate the results of simulating one hundred stops.
After conducting the simulation, the groups will respond to the following questions:

1. What percentage of the of the motorists pulled over by the
   CHP were Latinx?
2. What percentage of the motorists pulled over by the DHET
   were Latinx?
3. How did you set up the simulation for the investigation
   (how many "Latinx" cubes and how many total cubes)? Why
   did you choose those numbers?
4. In your simulation, how many Latinx were picked out of one
   hundred picks, and what percentage is that?
5. Do the results of the simulation investigation support the
   claim of racial profiling? Why or why not?

After the groups have had an opportunity to discuss their answers
to the questions, the group reporters will share their responses with
the whole class. The lesson ends with an individual journal reflection
responding to the following prompts:

1. What did you learn from this activity?

2. How did the mathematics help you do this?
3. Do you think racial profiling is a problem, and if so, what do you think should be done about it?
4. What questions does this project raise in your mind?

While there are many activities that could teach these probability concepts, activities like "Driving While Black or Brown" help solidify these ideas in students' minds because the context of the task is one that students can relate to. (Additional activities can be found in Appendix F.)

The Algebra Project

As teachers, we need to be able to help students go back and forth between school mathematics and real-world mathematics.[24] One example of how to do this is found in the work of Robert Moses. In the 1980s, Moses created a curriculum that would become the Algebra Project as a way to provide access to algebra for his daughter and the other students at her middle school, easing the transition from arithmetic to algebra by using a common activity in students' lives as context to deepen their quantitative reasoning.

The Algebra Project curriculum includes five essential steps:

1. **Physical Events:** Students share a common experience (such as a ride on the subway).
2. **Pictorial Representation/Modeling:** Students physically represent the experience using a visual model, such as a number line, graph, or diagram.
3. **Intuitive Language** (i.e., "People Talk"): Students write and talk about the experience in their own language.
4. **Structured Language** (i.e., "Feature Talk"): Students translate their own language into mathematical statements.

---

24 Robert P. Moses and Charles E. Cobb Jr., *Radical Equations: Math Literacy and Civil Rights* (Boston: Beacon Press, 2001).

5. **Symbolic Representation:** Students translate mathematical statements into mathematical notation.[25]

Here's how these essential steps played out in one lesson. Students took a subway ride from their school to a specific location and then returned to school. They took extensive notes about each stop, and when they returned to the classroom, they translated their trip notes into a number line and began to make sense of the idea that numbers have magnitude and directionality. This discussion then led into a lesson about positive and negative numbers and integer operations.

Bob Moses developed his curriculum to be successful with students who had a track record of math failure. Unlike with traditional programs that gave low-performing students a steady diet of remedial work, he believed that students in the lowest quartile would positively respond to a curriculum that was built on high expectations, shared experiences, and engagement in rich mathematical tasks based on those shared experiences. In a Cambridge study,[26] 92 percent of students taking the Algebra Project course in the eighth grade entered geometry the following year, which was twice the rate of their non–Algebra Project peers. Additionally, more than 60 percent of the Algebra Project students had passed trigonometry by the eleventh grade. The curriculum is hands-on and engaging, and it validates who students are as people. The curriculum is currently used in a variety of classrooms in districts across the United States and can be found at https://algebra.org/wp/.

---

25 Ibid.

26 M. West et al., *The Algebra Project's Middle School Intervention in 1997–98* (Cambridge, MA: Program Evaluation & Research Group, Lesley University, 1998).

— QUESTIONS TO CONSIDER —

1. In what ways can you help your students see themselves in the mathematics curriculum (e.g., textbooks, assessments, software, supplemental print and digital materials)?
2. How can you engage all students with the mathematics curriculum in ways that help them overcome negative stereotypes and messages regarding who is mathematically smart?

— CALL TO ACTION —

1. List the two ideas you learned from this chapter that are most relevant to your practice.
2. Complete the action plan below for each idea.

Idea 1:	
Vision for your students if you implement this idea in your classroom, school, or district	
Action step	
Deadline for action step	
Person you will ask to hold you accountable for completing this action step	

Idea 2:	
Vision for your students if you implement this idea in your classroom, school, or district	
Action step	
Deadline for action step	
Person you will ask to hold you accountable for completing this action step	

CHAPTER FIVE

ASSESS, ACTIVATE, AND BUILD ON PRIOR KNOWLEDGE

One of my greatest lesson flops turned out to be one of my most illuminating moments as an educator. I was teaching a lesson on piecewise functions to college freshmen in an Introduction to Math Modeling course. Because the course emphasized the real-life applications of the mathematics being taught, I wanted to help my students get a good understanding of how piecewise functions applied to the textbook example of health insurance deductibles. I spent hours creating spreadsheets and graphs that would illustrate different health care scenarios: the amount you pay when deductible hasn't been met (100%), amount you pay after deductible has been met (20%), and amount you pay after plan maximum has been met (0%). I showed up to class armed with tables and graphs and proceeded with my lesson. After making my presentation, I asked for questions. In response, I got the following: "What's a deductible?" "What's a plan maximum?" "How do you know when you've met the deductible or maximum?" I spent the rest of the class period explaining how health insurance works and never got a chance to answer any questions about piecewise functions.

Walking back to my office after class, I reflected on where I went wrong. Even though the textbook was full of real-life applications for the mathematical concepts, I forgot to ask, "Whose real life?" What do eighteen-year-olds who have just graduated from high school know about health insurance?

With that royal flop of a lesson still fresh in my mind, I started the next class session with a question. I drew a picture of a piecewise function and asked my students, "What does this remind you of?" One said it reminded him of a cell phone bill that is based upon how many minutes you use (he paid a flat rate until he went over his plan's allotment). Another was reminded of the amount of tuition she paid based upon the number of hours she took (more than twelve hours was a flat rate). I was pleasantly shocked at how quickly they were able to come up with examples that applied to their lives. That was how I learned that my effectiveness as a teacher is not dependent on my detailed notes but my ability to connect to the prior knowledge of my students!

— Pam

ASSESS, ACTIVATE, AND BUILD ON PRIOR KNOWLEDGE

Value the prior knowledge that students bring to the classroom, both personal and cultural, and leverage that knowledge as a resource for creating new knowledge.

Assessing prior knowledge is not only a best practice in education but an equity issue as well. Negative stereotypes and biases cause many teachers to wrongly assume their students have no prior knowledge about a topic and to make no attempts to find out if that is indeed the case. In her book, *Culturally Responsive Teaching and the Brain,* teacher educator Zaretta Hammond states that "all new information must be coupled with existing funds of knowledge in order to be learned."[1] Students who have backgrounds similar to those of their teachers will most likely experience having their background knowledge leveraged during instruction, especially for abstract mathematical concepts. When teachers do not value the prior knowledge of their students and fail to assess that prior knowledge, they are unable to use metaphors or analogies to connect to new math concepts. When students have the opportunity to draw on familiar cultural references to connect to math concepts, they are able to have more enduring understanding that significantly increases retention. Teachers who fail to identify prior knowledge, including misconceptions, at the beginning of instruction do so at the expense of their students' learning.

WHY ASSESSING, ACTIVATING, AND BUILDING ON PRIOR KNOWLEDGE IS AN EQUITY ISSUE

One of the reasons teachers often say their students don't know anything about the topic they are preparing to teach is because they don't value the informal knowledge students bring with them. For example, when introducing the topic of linear equations, teachers often begin instruction by teaching the steps for solving an equation—that is, first you add or subtract the same number from both sides, then you multiply or divide the same number from both sides, and so on. Very seldom do they stop to think about examples of when students reverse processes in real life, like putting on and taking off socks and shoes or loading and unloading groceries.

Lou Matthews, host of the *Pi Before Dinner* podcast, mentioned visiting a math classroom where a child walked up to him and introduced himself by his achievement level. For this student, his achievement level was such a part of his identity that he felt the need to include it when introducing himself to a stranger. The traditional

---

1   Zaretta Hammond, *Culturally Responsive Teaching and the Brain* (Thousand Oaks, CA: Corwin, 2015).

practice of using pre-assessment data to label students rather than for the purpose of creating new knowledge can be problematic. Studies show that labels themselves impact students' perceptions of their own abilities, so that students live up (or down) to the expectations of those labels.[2] Students identified as low, struggling, level 1, and so on tend to rise only to the expected level of performance set by their teachers and parents.

WHAT HAPPENS WHEN WE DON'T ASSESS, ACTIVATE, AND BUILD ON PRIOR KNOWLEDGE

Assessing is the process of collecting what students know. Teachers who fail to do this at the beginning of a unit can only make assumptions about what students know. There are consequences to assuming too little or too much.

Assuming too little

Teachers oftentimes don't pre-assess because they assume students don't know anything about the content to be taught. Assuming that students don't have the necessary prerequisites results in teachers wasting instructional time remediating students on topics they have already learned. A friend of Kyndall's worked at a high school that taught their algebra I course in ten-week segments. Starting at the beginning of the school year, students were taught the first ten weeks of algebra. If the students passed the first ten-week segment, they went on to the second ten-week segment. If they did not, they repeated that segment until they passed. The assumption with this model was that all students entered the class with the same knowledge, or lack thereof, and that they all needed the same instruction

---

2   Dara Shifrer, Rebecca Callahan, and Chandra Muller, "Equity or Marginalization? The High School Course-Taking of Students Labeled with a Learning Disability," *American Education Research Journal* 50, no. 4 (2013): 656–82, doi:10.3102/0002831213479439.

to be successful. There were many students who spent the first year of high school repeating the same ten-week algebra course over and over again. This had a devastating impact on their mathematical identities and sense of self-worth.

After teaching the same group of students for two ten-week segments in a row, Kyndall's friend noticed that many of the students had substantial algebraic knowledge, but not enough to successfully complete the ten-week course. On the third ten-week segment of the year, he decided to try something different. He administered a pre-assessment to all of his students to determine what concepts they had a solid grasp of and those that they still did not understand. With the results of the assessments, he was able to design his course to meet the individual needs of the students without using instructional time forcing them to sit through lessons on topics they already understood. Because he was able to build on students' prior knowledge, he was able to devote more time to topics they struggled with, and many of his repeating students passed the course and moved on to the next level. He was able to work around a curriculum designed with the assumption that students had none of the skills necessary for the course. His only regret was that he had not instituted his assessment strategy from the very beginning.

Assuming too much

Another consequence of failing to assess, activate, and build on prior knowledge is that some teachers assume that students have prerequisite knowledge they don't have. Because mathematics is sequential in nature, many new concepts students learn are built upon previous concepts. For example, in order for students to understand multiplication conceptually, they need to have a firm understanding of addition. Trying to teach multiplication to a student who does not understand addition will end in frustration for the teacher and the student. Making assumptions about what students know could lead to teachers lowering their expectations of student ability. The student who doesn't have the prior knowledge needed to access the content of the lesson is left feeling unintelligent and may blame themself for being the only one who does not understand. All of this turmoil can be avoided by the teacher if they incorporate formative assessment practices into their instruction.

Blaming others for knowledge gaps

There is a popular poem that begins with a college professor who complains about the lack of knowledge that his students have, blaming it on their high school teachers. The high school teachers, in turn, blame the middle school teachers, who blame the elementary school teachers. The elementary school teacher blames the mother, who then places responsibility on the father. The point of the poem is that everyone wants to pass blame to the person below them instead of taking responsibility for teaching students what they need to know to be successful now, in their own classes.

Teachers have no control over what learning experiences a student has had previously, so they need to accept that students enter their classrooms with different knowledge. The role of the teacher is to use assessment to determine student strengths and where any gaps may exist. They then need to use that information to design lessons that will fill the gaps while building new knowledge.

Not all teachers play the blame game. Some do take it upon themselves to go back and revisit previous grade-level content needed to learn new content. Others, however, seem to be annoyed that they have to return to previously learned concepts, and they communicate their disdain through their tone of voice or by making statements such as, "Didn't you learn this last year?" or "Didn't your teacher teach you this?" Students who are the recipients of this behavior are made to feel dumb and often shut down as a result. In urban schools that are predominately made up of students of color and from low socioeconomic backgrounds, learning gaps attributable to the education debt created from years of social, economic, and governmental neglect are more common. Teachers in these urban schools need to accept this reality, and, instead of getting annoyed and taking a deficit approach, they need to build a repertoire of strategies to effectively deal with it.

EFFECTIVELY ASSESSING, ACTIVATING, AND BUILDING ON PRIOR KNOWLEDGE

Culturally relevant teachers take the time to engage in formative assessment strategies that identify what students already know and identify gaps that could potentially hinder students in learning new math content. Rather than use these gaps as an excuse to stop teaching grade-level content to remediate, they build on that prior knowledge to introduce new concepts and use cooperative strategies that allow students to fill in the gaps where needed.

Education professor Jo Boaler recommends the use of low-floor, high-ceiling tasks.[3] These tasks are high level and cognitively demanding; however, they have multiple entry points, so all students can access the problem. For example, growth pattern tasks allow students to use their natural pattern recognition abilities to determine how a sequence continues to grow. Some students may count the figures in each shape and make a table. Other students may recognize the relationship between the figure number and the number of dots in the growth pattern and create a symbolic representation. Still others may create a graph to represent the relationship between the two variables in the problem. Tasks like these allow all students to participate at a level that matches their understanding and skill. They also serve as formative assessments for teachers to use, so they can build on students' strengths and help them make connections to other

---

3   Jo Boaler, *Mathematical Mindsets: Unleashing Students' Potential through Creative Math, Inspiring Messages, and Innovative Teaching* (San Francisco: Jossey-Bass, 2016).

representations that will advance their mathematical understanding. For example, two goals of an algebra I class are to get students to use algebraic symbols and graphs to represent the relationships between quantities. Teachers can use the representations that students create to describe the growth patterns to determine which students are fluent with symbolic and graphical representations and which are not and to help students see the connection between their representation and the symbolic and graphical representations.

Culturally relevant teachers also think about assessment of student knowledge in different ways. For example, in language arts classes, students are allowed to revise essay drafts after receiving their teacher's feedback. If they are to develop mathematical reasoning skills, mathematics students need to be given the same kinds of opportunities to revise their solutions to mathematics tasks. Rather than solely using assessment as a means to determine a student's grade, we should conduct assessments to determine students' prior knowledge and to assist in planning lessons. Students should have multiple opportunities to demonstrate their understanding of mathematical concepts. Students from marginalized groups are more able to overcome the impact of negative stereotypes when given the opportunity to learn from their mistakes in a nonpunitive way.

Amanda Jansen, a mathematics education researcher from the University of Delaware and author of *Rough Draft Math: Revising to Learn*,[4] sees the role of a teacher as shifting from an evaluator to someone who is making sense out of ideas with students. This begins with replacing procedural problems with tasks that ask students to explain their thinking. Rough draft thinking also expands the definition of what it means to be "smart" to include asking questions about someone's thinking, noticing how ideas are related, representing someone's thinking in a new way, or writing an explanation that makes more sense than the teacher's explanation. Another example

---

4   Amanda Jansen, *Rough Draft Math: Revising to Learn* (Portsmouth, NH: Stenhouse Publishers, 2020).

of rough draft thinking is having students share solution strategies before they are refined. Exams that allow students multiple opportunities to revise their thinking after receiving teacher feedback also engage students in rough draft thinking.

Students should also be taught how to self-assess their understanding of mathematical concepts in order to advocate for themselves. When students are able to self-assess, they are no longer reliant on others to validate their thinking. They can regulate their own learning and ask for assistance if needed.

Formative assessment refers to the process of gathering information about student thinking prior to and during instruction to make instructional decisions to guide students' learning.[5] Exit tickets are one example of a tool that can be used formatively in the mathematics classroom. With exit tickets, students respond to a prompt about the day's lesson before leaving class, which allows teachers to determine whether or not the students understood what was taught. Another example of an assessment tool that can be used formatively in the mathematics classroom is the use of whiteboards. Teachers pose a problem for students to solve on their whiteboards. When students have finished the problem, they hold up their whiteboards, which allows the teacher to determine whether or not the students understand the concept. Formative assessment strategies allow teachers to monitor student progress and modify instruction, as called for in *Principles to Actions*.[6] Research indicates that formative assessment improves instruction and results in some of the largest achievement gains reported for educational interventions. It is also useful in eliminating achievement and performance gaps.[7]

---

5   George Bright and Jeane Joyner, *INFORMative Assessment: Formative Assessment Practices to Improve Mathematics Achievement, Middle and High School* (Sausalito, CA: Math Solutions, 2016).

6   National Council of Teachers of Mathematics, *Principles to Actions: Ensuring Mathematics Success for All* (Reston, VA: NCTM, 2014).

7   Bright and Joyner, *INFORMative Assessment*.

Traditional mathematics instruction has relied on homework, quizzes, and tests to assess student understanding of mathematical concepts. As we move to a more culturally responsive method of teaching mathematics, there is a need to expand the repertoire of assessment techniques to determine what students know and are able to do.

Normalize filling in learning gaps

Many math teachers face the challenge of students who come to their classrooms with gaps in their mathematical understanding. When this happens, teachers have the option of taking a deficit approach to filling gaps, such as ability grouping, not engaging in grade-level content until students have "mastered basic skills," and sitting students at a computer to engage in rote drill and practice, all of which stigmatize students. But teachers can also address these gaps by using an assets-based approach, which can take on many forms. Students may be enrolled in an intervention block that allows them to acquire grade-level content along with their classmates but also receive additional support outside of class to learn concepts they may have missed. Another strategy is for teachers to incorporate regular review of fundamental concepts into their instruction, a process known as spiraling. Teachers can use instructional routines like "Which One Doesn't Belong," where students are given four numbers, shapes, equations, or graphs and have to choose which one of the four items doesn't belong. Teachers can make the four selections topics that students need more support with. One of the strengths of this activity is that there is no wrong answer. The important aspect of the routine is getting students to justify the choices they make.

Error analysis tasks, which allow students to look at the incorrect solution to a problem, identify where the error was made, correct the error, and determine the correct solution, are another way to fill gaps in student understanding by helping them recognize when they have made a mistake. (See p. 36 for a discussion on the role of error analysis in self-assessment.)

Math Password is another way to activate and build on prior knowledge. Not only is it very engaging because it's so much fun, but it also allows students to activate prior knowledge about terms they may have forgotten or learn new terms in an emotionally safe environment. Teachers can also determine students' depth of the understanding of these terms by the types of clues they give to their teammates.

Math Password—Vocabulary Game

Teacher Instructions: Divide students into groups of three or four and give each group a stack of vocabulary terms.

Student Instructions:

1. Select who will start with the first clue, and give that person the stack of math vocabulary terms face down so that no one can see the terms.
2. The first clue giver selects a math vocabulary term from the top of the stack and tries to describe it to the rest of the team without using any part of the term.
3. The first person who correctly guesses the term gets to keep that term.
4. Pass the stack of vocabulary terms clockwise to the next clue giver.
5. Repeat steps 2–4 until there are no cards left in the stack or until the teacher calls time.
6. The person with the most cards wins the game.

Sample Elementary Math Vocabulary Phrases

add	addend
associative property	commutative property
identity property	bar graph
difference	interval
picture graph	place value
round	scale
strategies	subtract
sum	plan
organize	evaluate

Sample Secondary Math Vocabulary Phrases

integer	exponent
equivalent expression	operation
scientific notation	equivalent equation
rational	irrational
dimensional analysis	polynomial
like terms	coefficient
transformation	reflection
complex number	conjugate
unit circle	radian

Connect new knowledge to prior knowledge

Culturally relevant teachers understand the importance of connecting new concepts to things that are already familiar to students. This is especially important in mathematics due to the abstract nature of many mathematical concepts. These teachers assume that all students bring knowledge, skills, and experiences, both personal and cultural, that should be used as resources in teaching and learning.[8] Douglas Hofstadter, a cognitive scientist at Indiana University Bloomington, says that "analogy is the engine of thinking." Simply asking students, "What is this like?" or "What does this make you think of?" can make them more determined to understand new content.[9]

One year, Pam observed that students in one of her classes took great pride in their communities, with many of them living in apartment complexes in neighborhoods in close proximity to the school. When she was teaching about the subsets of real numbers, she decided to use her students' neighborhoods as an analogy for the set of real numbers. She shared the diagram on page 126 to illustrate this relationship. Starlite Apartments is located in the Glenwood area of DeKalb County, which is located in north Georgia, just like natural numbers are a subset of whole numbers, which are a subset of integers. Because she was able to connect these abstract mathematical concepts to something students were already very familiar with, they were able to make the necessary connections to truly understand and retain the material.

---

8   Kenneth M. Zeichner et al. "A Research Informed Vision of Good Practice in Multicultural Teacher Education: Design Principles," *Theory into Practice* 37, no. 2 (1998): 163–71.

9   Douglas Hofstadter, "Analogy as the Core of Cognition," in *The Analogical Mind: Perspectives from Cognitive Science,* ed. Dedre Gentner et al. (Cambridge, MA: MIT Press/Bradford Book, 2001), 499–538.

The Set of Real Numbers

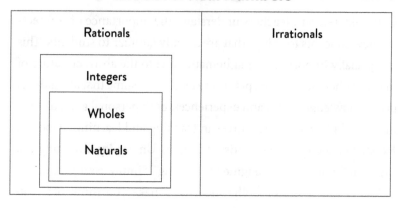

Georgia

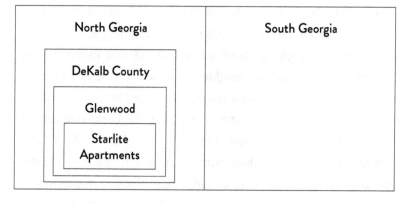

Another method you can use to connect prior knowledge to new knowledge is to project a picture or graph related to the day's topic and ask students to write down the following:

1. Five factual statements about the picture.
2. Two questions they have about the picture.

The first requirement assesses and activates their prior knowledge. Once students have finished writing down their observations and questions, you can randomly call on students to share their factual statements with the class. Record all of the answers on the board, and accept all statements without judgment. Alternatively, give students sticky notes to write their responses on, and arrange all of them on the board or have students take turns reading them out loud to the class. At this point, it is critical not to evaluate their statements so you can hear from as many students as possible. Many students will not risk sharing their statements if they feel they will immediately be critiqued.

Some of your students may complain that they could only think of two or three observations, not five. Insisting on five, however, will cause them to look beyond surface details, as well as dig deeper into their memories to access prior knowledge. When they share their responses, you can ask that students not repeat an answer that has already been given. Most will be excited to share their statements, and the no repetition rule will make them think harder.

Next, use students' questions about the picture as a segue to the day's topic. You are likely to find that by beginning the lesson with their questions, they will be so much more motivated to learn. When we've done this activity with our students, we have often been delighted by how clearly their questions aligned to the lesson goals. It's even more exciting when students come up with questions you hadn't previously considered. You can use these to develop ideas for enrichment activities that your students are sure to be motivated to complete because they will be based on their own questions.

At the end of the lesson, you can revisit the original statements and ask students to respond by saying, "I agree, because ..." or "I disagree, because . . ." You may even want to add in your own statement that will uncover a common misconception about the lesson topic to see if students' understanding has grown over the course of the lesson.

Equity-based lesson study

For the last three years, Kyndall has been involved with a grant-funded project exploring equity-based lesson study that has helped teachers connect to students' prior knowledge. Lesson study is a form of structured, collaborative lesson planning that is teacher driven and student focused. Teams of teachers work together to plan and teach a lesson. Then they observe one another teaching the lesson and provide feedback on student learning. In our model of lesson study, teachers choose three or four focal students, students who have not been performing well in mathematics. Each teacher on the team interviews their focal students to find out more about their mathematical identity and agency. The interview, which also includes having the student complete a mathematics task and explain their thinking, consists of the following questions:

1. What is mathematics? Can you describe mathematics? How and when do you use mathematics outside of school?

2. What do successful mathematics students do when working on mathematics problems? What are they thinking about? Talking about? Whose ideas are being used? How? Are your ideas used? How? Say more.

3. How do you work on challenging mathematics problems? What makes problems challenging for you? Can you give me an example of a challenging problem? How might you start to solve this problem? What do you do when you get stuck? How do you know if you have the right answer? Do you like challenging problems? Why? Why not?

4. Can you get better at mathematics? How? Can students get better at mathematics? What do you need to do? What support would you like in order to get better?

5. How does your family use mathematics? At home? Work? Out and about?

The responses to these questions are used to write assets-based descriptions of students and to develop equity goals for the mathematics lesson. An example of an equity goal written by a lesson study team is, "We will build students' agency as math learners who feel confident in expressing their mathematical thinking, making sense of others' ideas, and constructing understanding." These focal student descriptions include the academic challenges, as well as conceptual strengths, that can be built upon. Teachers use these descriptions to design a lesson to specifically meet the needs of their focal students in ways that connect the content they are teaching to the prior understandings and dispositions of the focal students. One of the teachers on the team then teaches this collaboratively designed lesson while the rest of the team observes. In our model, we also have incorporated the use of two outside experts, called commentators. One of the commentators observes the lesson for the mathematics content, the other commentator observes the lesson to determine the extent to which the equity goals for the lesson were met.

After the lesson has been taught, there is a debrief. The teacher who taught the lesson and the team that designed the lesson have an opportunity to share their thoughts about the lesson implementation. Next, the commentators share their observations on the lesson. The planning team may then use the feedback to redesign and reteach the lesson.

We have found that the process of interviewing and designing a lesson to meet the needs of focal students has a profound impact on students and teachers. For most of the students, it was the first time a teacher took the time to ask them about their mathematical thinking. Lessons are designed in ways that ensure the focal student is able to participate and share their thinking, whether it is with other students in pairs or groups or with the whole class during a share-out. I have witnessed focal students who were described as introverted and who never shared their thinking challenge another student's strategy in a small group or project their solution to a problem on a screen or whiteboard using a document camera and explain what they did to the class.

For the teachers, the process of interviewing a student and designing a lesson to meet their needs helps them to move past stereotypes, labels, and deficit thinking. When teachers see the focal student successfully engaging in a mathematics task, it changes their perception of that student. The changes they see in the student's performance help to develop teacher agency, in that teachers now have evidence that changing their practice can have a positive impact on student learning.

— QUESTIONS TO CONSIDER —

1. How can *not* taking the time to assess or activate the prior knowledge of your students perpetuate inequities in your classroom?
2. What analogies can you use to help connect students' prior knowledge to abstract math concepts?

— CALL TO ACTION —

1. List the two ideas you learned from this chapter that are most relevant to your practice.
2. Complete the action plan on the following page for each idea.

Idea 1:	
Vision for your students if you implement this idea in your classroom, school, or district	
Action step	
Deadline for action step	
Person you will ask to hold you accountable for completing this action step	

Idea 2 :	
Vision for your students if you implement this idea in your classroom, school, or district	
Action step	
Deadline for action step	
Person you will ask to hold you accountable for completing this action step	

CHAPTER SIX

RELEASE CONTROL

Ivan was a student in my precalculus class. He was a friendly young man who always came to class and put in his best effort. He turned in his homework on a regular basis. The challenge I faced with Ivan was that he could never pass my chapter tests. I always gave students an entire class period to complete a chapter test. One day, when I was administering one of these tests, the bell rang for the end of class. All of the students turned in their tests. Ivan approached me to ask if he could have more time to finish his test. It was the last period of the day, and I usually stayed after school to finish grading the tests, so I told Ivan that he could stay and finish. Ivan stayed for another forty-five minutes to work on his test and then turned it in to me. Later that day, I graded it. To my astonishment, he got about 90 percent of the questions correct, getting his first A. It dawned on me that Ivan was perfectly capable of passing my tests; he simply needed more time. I felt so guilty that I had given Ivan a lower grade than he deserved because I had not given him enough time. From that point on, one of my policies around tests was permanently changed: I always give students as much time as they need to take a test. This experience has also caused me to question the value of timed tests in general.

— Kyndall —

RELEASE CONTROL

Empower your students to take ownership of their learning by focusing on sensemaking and allow them to make choices about things that are important to them in the classroom.

Teachers often fear that if they are not in "control," students will engage in behaviors that will undermine the learning environment. Releasing control is not about letting students do whatever they want in the name of freedom and liberation. It must be coupled with high expectations. What we are proposing is that everyone shares the responsibility. Teachers are responsible for establishing rituals and routines that help students be accountable to each other for maintaining a positive, supportive environment. The emphasis should be on empowerment through cooperation, not compliance.

Culturally relevant teachers seek to redistribute power and privilege in their classrooms by sharing these with their students. They act as gate openers, rather than gatekeepers, by facilitating critical thinking and helping all students see themselves as constructors of knowledge. Two things must happen for this redistribution of power to occur: (1) Teachers must shift the focus of mathematics instruction away from answer-getting techniques to focus on sensemaking, and (2) Teachers must give students choices about what they learn and how they learn in the classroom. Culturally relevant teachers understand the need to effectively balance decentralized control and accountability. Rather than making students accountable to the teacher, culturally relevant teachers engage in strategies that hold students accountable to each other.

WHY RELEASING CONTROL
IS AN EQUITY ISSUE

Critical theory is a social philosophy that is based on the idea that political and economic power are unequally and unjustly distributed in society and therefore subject to critique.[1] Traditional classroom structures that prioritize order and control often serve to preserve the inequities already prevalent in society at large. This is especially the case in low-performing schools in poor neighborhoods with high concentrations of students of color, where teachers maintain control by doing most of the talking in class and students passively take notes. The following sections further describe ways that traditional schooling structures and practices that prioritize order and control continue to perpetuate inequity along racial, ethnic, and socioeconomic lines.

CRITICAL THEORY IN EDUCATION

Socioeconomic class and education inequity

Education researcher Jean Anyon's 1980 article, "Social Class and the Hidden Curriculum of Work," illustrates how schooling reproduces the social class structures of the communities where the schools are located. Anyon studied schools in New Jersey and classified them as working class, middle class, affluent professional, and executive elite. In working-class schools, the majority of work is about following procedures. In middle-class schools, the emphasis is on getting the right answer. In affluent professional schools, the work is centered around creative activity done independently. In executive elite schools, students are allowed to develop their analytical intellectual

---

1   George M. A. Stanic, "Social Inequality, Cultural Discontinuity, and Equity in School Mathematics," *Peabody Journal of Education* 66, no. 2 (1991): 57–71.

powers.[2] Even though this research is forty years old, as we work with teachers in schools, we still see the same patterns of instruction with respect to socioeconomic status. Anyon's research indicates that the poorer the students are, the less likely they are to have teachers who release control. Given the fact that people of color are more prone to live in working-class or middle-class neighborhoods, it is reasonable to assume that they will more often have teachers who do not release control.

The banking system of education

According to the Brazilian philosopher and educator Paulo Freire, education serves the interest of oppression (overwhelming control) when it attempts to control thinking and action by transforming students into receiving objects, inhibiting their creative power.[3] In his "banking" concept of education, students, who know nothing, are mere receptacles for the teacher's knowledge, which is patiently received, memorized, and repeated. Under this system, the all-knowing teacher does the talking and thinking, while students passively listen and/or regurgitate information that was deposited by the teacher. The teacher chooses program content without consulting the students, and students adapt to it. The teacher enforces his/her will through discipline and grading, and the students comply.

In his research with poor children in urban schools, Martin Haberman documented activities prevalent in this system of education as follows:
- Giving information and directions
- Asking yes or no questions
- Monitoring seatwork
- Giving and reviewing tests

2   Jean Anyon, "Social Class and the Hidden Curriculum of Work," *Journal of Education* 162, no. 1 (1980): 67–92.

3   Paulo Freire, *Pedagogy of the Oppressed*, 30th anniversary ed. (New York: Continuum, 2000).

- Assigning and reviewing homework
- Settling disputes
- Punishing noncompliance
- Marking papers and giving grades[4]

When Kyndall first read this list when he was still a classroom teacher, he was appalled to realize these were the primary aspects of his own instructional routine. He recognized that he needed to change his teaching practices if he was going to help his students become mathematically powerful. He thus sought out professional learning experiences to make his teaching more student centered. You may also recognize some of your own practices in this list.

Because recipients of this form of education are more likely to accept the passive role imposed upon them, they are less likely to become transformers of the system, which is presented to them as just and fair. The banking system of education mirrors the political system of oppression by communicating to the members of marginalized groups that the current reality is the normal order of things. Just like the teacher is always right and unchallengeable, the government (along with its political systems) is always right and not to be challenged.

Since those with political power have too much at stake and too much to lose to change the system, Freire asserts that marginalized groups need a pedagogy that will liberate them from their current condition of oppression. He proposes replacing the banking system of education with "problem-posing" education, where both students and teachers become jointly responsible for the teaching and learning process through dialogue.

---

4   Martin Haberman, "The Pedagogy of Poverty versus Good Teaching," *Phi Delta Kappa* 92, no. 2 (2010): 81–87.

Preserving current inequities

Teachers who don't release control see themselves as the sole authority in the classroom. This type of teacher usually decides how lessons are taught, what assignments are given, and how knowledge is assessed without any input from students, parents, or even other teachers. It is the teacher who chooses whether or not students collaborate.

While it is important for a teacher to maintain authority for the purposes of classroom management, there are ways to share authority with students in ways that help build their identities and still allow for a productive learning environment. As students proceed through the mathematics curriculum, they will be expected to engage in critical thinking, problem solving, mathematical modeling, and proof. The only way that students are going to be able to engage in these types of practices is for teachers at all levels to allow students to partake in collaborative problem solving. This means the teacher must surrender an amount of authority so students can learn how to ask mathematical questions, make and test conjectures, and challenge each other's ideas. This also means reassessing the types of tasks you assign (drill-and-practice versus open-ended tasks), the ways you assess students (multiple choice/short answer tests and quizzes versus performance tasks), and grading policies (curves and percentages versus mastery grading).

Lack of agency

Too many students, particularly low-income students of color, do not get opportunities to explain and present their mathematical ideas. Alan Schoenfeld, professor of education and mathematics at the University of California, Berkeley, includes agency, identity, and ownership as one of the five dimensions of mathematically powerful classrooms. These represent "the extent to which students are provided opportunities to contribute to conversations about mathematical ideas, to build on others' ideas and have others build on theirs in ways that contribute to their agency."[5]

For Kyndall's dissertation study, he taught a culturally centered mathematics enrichment class for African American and Latinx male students. A regular feature of the class was a problem of the day. Every day, he chose a couple of students to come to the front of the room and share their solutions with the class. One day, after a student shared his solution, he informed Kyndall that it was the first time he had ever presented in front of a class.

When teachers allow students to share their thinking with others, it contributes to students' confidence in their own ability to reason. When students are not recognized as being capable and able to share their ideas in meaningful ways, they remain dependent on their teachers and the "smart" students to validate their thinking.

Gatekeeping of higher-level mathematics

Akil was a student taking precalculus in his sophomore year of high school. In the first semester, he received a grade of C, and in the second semester, he received a B. In order to take AP Calculus, the school required students to get a recommendation letter signed by their precalculus teacher. When Akil asked his teacher to sign his permission slip, she refused, saying that she did not think he was mature enough for AP Calculus.

Akil's father met with the school principal to complain. The principal reassured the father that Akil would be able to take the class the following year despite the actions of his precalculus teacher. However, before the principal could act, Akil approached his teacher to state his case as to why she should sign his permission slip. He explained that there were students who had performed the same as or worse than he did whose permission slips she signed. After

---

5   A. Schoenfeld, "Teaching for Robust Understanding," *Mathematics Assessment Resource Center*, https://www.map.mathshell.org/trumath.php.

listening to his argument, the teacher agreed to sign his permission slip, and Akil went on to successfully pass AP Calculus.

Akil's story is just one example of a teacher serving as a gatekeeper, something that happens every day in America's schools. Fortunately, Akil had not only a supportive parent but also the agency to advocate for himself. When students don't have advocates or agency, they are often subject to the whims of teachers who don't believe in their abilities.

WHAT HAPPENS WHEN WE RESIST RELEASING CONTROL

Teachers tend not to delegate authority because they are convinced that without constant, direct supervision their classes will descend into chaos and their students won't know what to do, will make too many mistakes, won't complete their assignments, and will disengage from learning mathematics altogether. The overemphasis on standardized testing has been a catalyst for this fear. When teacher evaluations are dependent upon student scores on state tests, it is easy to understand why fear would be so pervasive in schools, especially in the lowest-performing schools. Instead of creating environments that are emotionally safe for learning, the culture of blame that has resulted from the overemphasis on standardized testing has undermined learning for both teachers and students.

Prioritizing order over learning

One sign of the prioritization of order over learning is the amount of time and energy invested in preventing students from cheating. We've seen teachers only assign the even problems for independent practice so students won't "cheat" by copying the answers from the back of the book. We are saddened that teachers would rob students of the opportunity to self-assess and self-correct because of their fear they might cheat. When students were suddenly forced to engage in remote learning due to the COVID-19 pandemic, it was amazing how many teachers and leaders kept asking the question, "How do we keep students from cheating by googling the answers to their assignments?"

Our response is that we can't. The need to control students keeps the focus on the wrong question. As educators who are interested in equitable mathematics instruction, we should be asking, "How do we ask questions in ways that cheating doesn't benefit students? How do we meaningfully engage our students with mathematics so they don't want to cheat because they genuinely want to learn what we have to offer?" All of our students, but especially students from marginalized groups, will benefit the most from us putting our time, energy, and resources into answering these questions.

Stifling of students' natural learning processes

It is amazing how much children learn before they ever set foot into a school. Their natural curiosity to make sense of their world through inquiry and exploration yields a great acceleration of learning in a child's early years. Unfortunately, traditional mathematics instruction does not take advantage of those natural learning processes but often actually undermines them by insisting that students learn to memorize routines and procedures that make no sense to them. This is especially true if mathematics is taught in ways that do not align with a student's culture. For example, if your culture encourages and celebrates collaboration, then classes that emphasize working in isolation to prevent cheating can put you at a great disadvantage.

Because many teachers' identities are so tied to their students' ability to get good grades, they're often socialized to take on more and more of the responsibility of learning from their students. In an effort to help students get more right answers, well-intentioned teachers often give too much help, provide too much information, and do too much of the thinking for struggling learners. In the short run, it does provide more right answers, and sometimes better grades, but it most often results in less learning and less understanding. This desire to be perceived as a good teacher with students who make good grades often comes at the expense of students' long-term learning and understanding. Unfortunately, the mathematical gaps that are created by the mindless following of rules often do not show up until middle or high school. Nonetheless, these procedures are too often imposed upon students through the power structure of schooling and well-meaning teachers.

Undermining student motivation

Students who have little input in what mathematics they study and how they study it are often unmotivated to learn it. Too often mathematics is wielded like a sword, bestowing rewards on those who quickly reproduce mathematical procedures with correct answers and traumatizing those considered deficient and devalued because of wrong answers. Rather than encouraging public sharing of thought processes for the good of the whole, teachers further traumatize students with the labels they place on those who cannot or will not produce the answers that fit into their detailed lesson plans. As a result of a "banking" system of education, many students choose compliance over meaningful learning by asking themselves, "What do I need to do to pass?"

So many practices that teachers engage in are dehumanizing. When Kyndall visited mathematics classrooms in a local school district as part of a professional development contract, he found himself sitting in an algebra II class where the teacher was going over the answers to an assignment. For each problem, the teacher called on a student to share their answer. When a student gave a correct answer, the teacher acknowledged the answer and proceeded to call on another student. One student started to explain her solution to a problem, but before she could finish, the teacher shouted, "WRONG!" You could feel the mood of the class change. Instead of allowing the student to fully explain her answer to understand her thinking, the teacher shut her down. The message all of the students received that day was that only correct answers matter and that mistakes are a bad thing.

Learning to release control

I still remember the pain I felt when one of my students told me how much he hated my class. I was both hurt and embarrassed. It was the end of my first year of teaching, and I had asked my students to complete a course evaluation. Since this had been common practice in my college classes, I didn't think it was strange to do with my high school students. However, I was not prepared for the results. Although most of the evaluations were positive, the level of negative emotion this particular student shared in writing hit me especially hard. Because I had made the conscious decision not to make the evaluations anonymous and to give them a few days before school was out, I decided to talk to this student in private about his experience in my class.

When I told him that I wanted to talk with him about his evaluation, he thought he was in trouble. I assured him that he was not, but that I genuinely wanted to learn from him about why his experience in my math class was so negative. He explained to me that his venting on the evaluation was not a true reflection of all that he had experienced, but he did give some suggestions for ways I could improve. His main frustration was that he felt like he had very few choices about what he learned and how he learned it. I thanked him for his honesty and assured him that there would be no negative repercussions as a result of our conversation.

I was struck by his fear of providing me honest feedback. He didn't think that the feedback was for me, but rather for the administration. As a first-year teacher who was really trying to learn how to be better, it didn't cross my mind that getting feedback from students would be so counter to *the culture of schooling. In traditional school settings, it was the job of the teacher to critique the students—not the other way around! Apparently, no other teachers had ever voluntarily asked for his feedback on their teaching practices. I was sad this student had had such a negative experience in my class and that I did not know it until the end of the year. If I hadn't given the student survey, I would have never known! Even though it was painful, I am so grateful that this experience happened my first year of teaching. I learned an invaluable lesson about the importance of student voice and how I needed my students to teach me how to be a better teacher.*

Pam

One of the challenges that mathematics educators face is trying to develop critical thinking skills in students using banking methodologies. It doesn't work. Students who are taught to passively receive abstract information, rules, and procedures apart from their own realities are not being prepared to engage in critical inquiry or problem solving. Releasing control means that the roles of teachers and learners are interconnected and inseparable. Yes, we know that young people need teachers to teach them how to be effective students. Students don't always know how to study (especially for math class), how to take notes, how to prepare for exams, and how to effectively communicate what they know. Teachers must take responsibility for explicitly teaching all these skills. More often than not, teachers don't think about how they need students to teach them how to be effective teachers. This is where sharing of power is critical for marginalized students. Very rarely do teachers ask students for advice on teaching. Who better to give that advice than the recipient of the teacher's instruction?

Disrupting classroom power dynamics

Sometimes teachers are reluctant to release control in their classrooms because of past experiences with students engaging in negative behaviors while working in groups, such as calling each other dumb or stupid or insinuating that their peers don't know what they are talking about. Explicitly teaching students cooperative group norms and student roles can help teachers delegate authority.[6] It is especially important to help students avoid negative, insensitive behaviors while working in groups by investing in team building, desirable group processes, and feedback on cooperative behaviors specifically tied to the mathematics task they are engaging in.

Two good resources that provide guidance for roles are Elizabeth Cohen and Rachel Lotan's complex instruction and *Kagan Cooperative Learning* roles.[7] The *Kagan Cooperative Learning* strategy Rally Coach structures the interaction between students so that each student is expected to learn how to complete every problem as well as ensure his/her partner understands the problems. During this activity, teachers turn their coaching roles over to students. The power of this activity is that every student gets the benefit of giving and receiving coaching, thus disrupting the power dynamic normalized in most classrooms.

Rally Coach

Before introducing Rally Coach, complete the following T-chart as a class. Students should be given the opportunity to come up with their own answers to these questions. The teacher's role is to record their responses on the chart, and then post the chart in the classroom for students to refer to as needed.

---

6   Elizabeth Cohen and Rachel Lotan, "Equity in Heterogeneous Classrooms," in *Handbook of Research on Multicultural Education*, 2nd ed., ed. James A. Banks and Cherry A. McGee Banks (San Francisco: Jossey-Bass, 2003).

7   Spencer Kagan and Miguel Kagan, *Kagan Cooperative Learning* (San Clemente, CA: Kagan Publishing, 2009).

What does good coaching look like? (*Things you see*)	What does good coaching sound like? (*Things you hear*)
Interested looks on faces Smiles Bodies turned toward partner Pencils in the hand of the person working the problem	Questions being asked Hints or clues being given "Good job!" "Try again." "Are you sure?" "Check your answer." "How do you know?"

What does bad coaching look like? (*Things you see*)	What does bad coaching sound like? (*Things you hear*)
Looking away from partner Body language that communicates anger, such as frowns, fists, violating personal space, etc. Bodies turned away from partner Pencils being taken from the person working the problem	Telling, not asking Words such as "dumb," "stupid," and "wrong." "Let me do it." "Since you can't do this, I will."

Teacher Instructions:

1. Divide the class into pairs.
2. Make sure each pair shares the same paper and same pen/pencil.

Student Instructions:

1. Agree on who will be Person A and Person B.
2. Person A works problem 1 while Person B coaches.

3. Person B verifies that the problem was done correctly by placing their initials next to the problem.

4. Person B works problem 2 while Person A coaches.

5. Person A verifies that the problem was done correctly by placing their initials next to the problem.

6. Repeat steps 2–5 with Person A completing the odd problems while Person B coaches, and Person B completing the even problems while Person A coaches.

Shifting focus from answer-getting to sensemaking

During the No Child Left Behind (NCLB) era, schools were rewarded when their standardized test scores rose and penalized when they fell. As a result, many schools resorted to an emphasis on teaching their students basic skills as a way to prepare them for standardized testing. Teachers fell into the trap of thinking that "telling is teaching" and that students could not learn vocabulary and/or formulas without teachers explicitly telling them what they should know. A popular, teacher-centered instructional model, Explicit Direct Instruction (EDI), was adopted by many schools and teachers. Teachers would present information about a topic, model how to apply that information to various problems, and then ask students to put into practice the processes modeled to them with the support of classmates or the teacher. Last, students would be expected to perform the previously modeled processes independently on worksheets or textbook problems for homework. Also known as Gradual Release of Responsibility, the common description for EDI was "I do, we do, you do." The model became problematic when students encountered a problem that involved a process that had not already been modeled by the teacher. While research has indicated that EDI is a way to improve standardized test scores, there are no data to suggest that it helps students improve their critical-thinking and problem-solving skills. The problem with this model is that it begins with the teacher, not the student.

As mentioned in the previous chapter, we believe that good instruction begins with assessing, activating, and building on student's prior knowledge, not with the information that teachers want students to know. Therefore, we recommend that teachers release control by giving students the opportunity to make sense of the mathematics before they start presenting vocabulary and formulas. By adding a "You do, we do" component in front of the "I do, we do, you do," teachers can make their lessons more student centered. One way to do this is to provide students with something related to the topic and ask students to write down things they notice and wonder about the item. For example, before a lesson on measurement, students can be given a ruler and asked to write down five things they notice about the ruler and one question they have about it. After recording their observations and questions individually, they can compare their responses with those of a partner or teammates. After the teacher has given students the opportunity to share their observations and questions with the class, the teacher can then build upon that shared knowledge to present a lesson on measurement. Teachers can begin this process with an image, graph, tool, video, game, or problem that is connected to the lesson. The diagram on the next page illustrates this process.

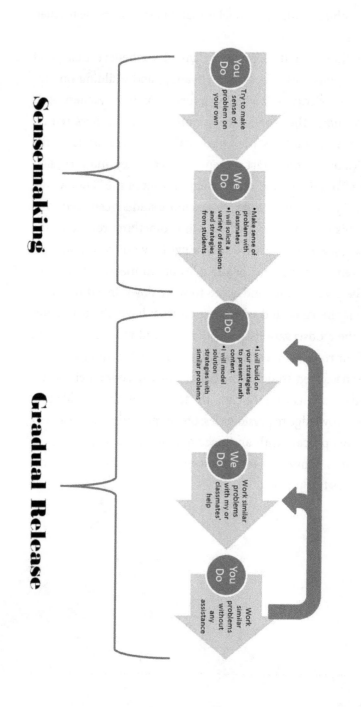

Instructional Progression for Math

Sensemaking

Gradual Release

You Do — Try to make sense of problem on your own

We Do — Make sense of problem with classmates • I will solicit a variety of solutions and strategies from students

I Do — I will build on your strategies to present math content • I will model solution strategies with similar problems

We Do — Work similar problems with my or classmates' help

You Do — Work similar problems without any assistance

Another way to provide students with sensemaking activities before explicit instruction is with card sorts, an activity that involves students sorting a set of cards into groups that make sense to them. It could be a set of vocabulary words, various equations, shapes, graphs, or anything else that fits the lesson. When students have the opportunity to share their sorting methods with classmates, the teacher is better able to provide instruction that is focused on conceptual understanding, rather than rule following or answer getting.

A card sort activity that Pam has used frequently with her students is based on the idea that a math concept can be represented in a variety of ways. For example, a subtraction problem can be represented with words (I have five dollars and gave two dollars to a friend), with symbols (5 − 2), with a number (3), or with an image ($ $ $ $–$). Mathematically proficient students are able to flexibly translate between multiple representations. A teacher would have to model twelve different procedures if they were to explicitly teach students all the ways they could translate between the various representations of this subtraction problem (e.g., words to symbols, words to image, symbols to numbers, symbols to images). Even if the teacher were to model all twelve procedures, the students would most likely confuse them if they are not provided opportunities to see how these various representations are connected. That is where the card sort comes in. Asking students to match a set of cards with problems represented verbally, abstractly, numerically, and graphically can help students make those connections on their own, especially if they explain the methods they use to match the cards with their classmates.

The VANG game is an example of a card sort that has been turned into a game format, where students match the **V**erbal (words), **A**bstract (equation), **N**umerical (numbers), and **G**raphical (image) representations of the same math idea. The following is an example where the four cards represent the same fraction concept in four different ways.

The total hours you studied if you spent three-halves hours studying on Monday and one-third of an hour on Tuesday.	n = 3/2 + 1/3	11/6 or 1 5/6	

Multiple representations of three-halves plus one-third

The game has twelve sets of cards that match. When students play the matching game to determine which cards go together, they begin to make subtle distinctions without direct instruction from the teacher. Rather than being given specific instructions for going from words to an equation to a number, students are able to start with the representation they are most comfortable with and make connections in the order that makes the most sense to them. It is amazing the number of "aha" moments that happen when students collaboratively match these cards and then are provided time to share their thinking about how they grouped the cards. Pam noticed that when her students played the VANG game, they were more willing to try procedures that were unfamiliar to them, more willing to help each other, and more willing to put in the time needed to master a concept. Resisting the urge to tell students explicitly how to go from one representation to another really pays off for students.

Offering choices

Many times, teachers are afraid to call on a student they perceive as low achieving out of fear they will embarrass them if they don't know an answer. Asking questions that have no right or wrong answers, like "How did you think about this problem?" or "Name three things you observe about this graph," is one way to alleviate this problem. In traditional classrooms where correctly answering the teacher's questions is a hallmark of intelligence, students who publicly give a wrong answer fear getting that dreaded label of being dumb. When students matriculate through schooling structures that foster fixed mindsets through competition and an emphasis on right answers and looking smart, they learn to avoid looking dumb at all costs—even if that means not trying at all. Allowing students to choose board buddies when asked questions in class can go a long way to helping alleviate a student's fear and embarrassment of looking dumb because they can't immediately answer the teacher's questions. A board buddy is any person in the classroom whom a student chooses to help them when the teacher asks them to go to the board to answer a question. This strategy also works during class discussions or any other time students are called on in class to publicly answer a question. When teachers establish this system as routine in their classrooms, asking for help is normalized, and students are accountable to paying attention to their classmates in case they are asked to be someone's board buddy.

Choice boards are another great option. A choice board is a graphic organizer that allows students to choose how they will learn or demonstrate mastery of a topic. Three benefits of using choice boards are that they (1) increase students' intrinsic motivation, (2) address various learning preferences, and (3) provide differentiated learning opportunities.[8] The Totally Ten Choice Board can be used for independent practice or for any assessments. Allowing students to choose how to show what they know is especially important for those from marginalized groups who often have to fight the preconceived notions that, if they can't answer questions in a specific and rigid way, they aren't smart. Choice boards lower anxiety because students can start with problems they easily know, which often builds their confidence for tackling more difficult problems. Students

---

8 Kristen Yann, "3 Reasons to Use Choice Boards in Your Classroom," *School and the City,* July 3, 2020, https://satcblog.com/3-reasons-to-use-choice-boards-in-your/.

choose the questions, worth varying number of points, they want to answer, as long as their points total to a certain number. Teachers can specify that students choose at least one question for each level.

Elementary Totally Ten Quiz

Directions: You may choose problems from any category to total a score of 10. You may pick only two problems from the Score 2 section. For example, you may choose 1 Score 2 problem, and 1 Score 8 problem, or you may choose 2 Score 2 problems and 1 Score 6 problem. The choice is yours! For extra credit, you may earn a maximum score of 12. SHOW ALL WORK on a separate piece of paper.

Score 2 Evaluate: 25 + 32 Evaluate: 45 – 27 Evaluate: 17 × 26
Score 4 Create an addition problem that will result in the following answer: 833 Create a subtraction problem that will result in the following answer: 211 Create a multiplication problem that will result in the following answer: 544
Score 6 Create a division word problem that will result in the following answer: 13
Score 8 Create a problem for each operation (addition, subtraction, multiplication, and division) that will result in the following answer: 242

Secondary Totally Ten Quiz

Score 2 Simplify: $(6x - 2) + (9x^2 + 6x)$ Simplify: $(4x^2 - 5) - (x^2 + 2x - 7)$ Simplify: $-7x^2 y(3x^2 y - 2xy^2 - 6y^3)$
Score 4 Create an addition polynomial problem that will result in the following answer: $8a^2 + 3a + 3$ Create a subtraction polynomial problem that will result in the following answer: $-5c^3 + 2c^2 - c + 11$ Create a multiplication polynomial problem that will result in the following answer: $72b^2 - 119b + 49$
Score 6 Create a volume polynomial problem that will result in the following answer: $2s^3 + 13s^2 + 6s$
Score 8 Create a polynomial problem for each operation (addition, subtraction, multiplication, and division) that will result in the following answer: $2x^3 + 13x^2 - x + 42$

— QUESTIONS TO CONSIDER —

1. What keeps you from giving more control to your students for their learning? How can you overcome these obstacles?
2. How can you remove the fear of making mistakes from your classroom?
3. What structures/routines in your classroom might communicate that the answer is more important than the process?
4. How might you modify those structures/routines to promote sensemaking?

— CALL TO ACTION —

1. List the two ideas you learned from this chapter that are most relevant to your practice.
2. Complete the action plan below for each idea.

Idea 1:	
Vision for your students if you implement this idea in your classroom, school, or district	
Action step	
Deadline for action step	
Person you will ask to hold you accountable for completing this action step	

Idea 2 :	
Vision for your students if you implement this idea in your classroom, school, or district	
Action step	
Deadline for action step	
Person you will ask to hold you accountable for completing this action step	

CHAPTER SEVEN

EXPECT MORE

I once served as an instructional coach at an alternative school to which students had been assigned because of past discipline issues, including truancy. On several occasions, I observed students who were very disengaged, even though the teachers really had a desire to reach them. I suggested that the teacher try using technology to get students hooked into the lesson. In the file cabinet were graphing calculators that had never been used, still in the original packaging. The teacher indicated that he did not want his students to use graphing calculators until they had learned how to graph by hand. I convinced him to let me teach his class, and I began the period by telling the students that I needed their help with the graphing calculators. After they had taken them out of the plastic and inserted batteries, the students were quite interested in figuring out how these new calculators worked.

I then gave them an activity that asked them to enter values from a table to determine how much a crate of oranges would weigh. With assistance from their classmates and me, they figured out how to determine the weight of the crate of oranges using the calculators' graphing features and the corresponding equation to the graph. They noticed that the initial weight of the crate without any oranges represented the y-intercept and that the average weight of one orange represented the slope. I then asked them to create graphs that represented crates with oranges of various amounts. Through trial and error, the students were able to successfully represent the various scenarios graphically by entering the corresponding equations into the graphing calculator. When I debriefed the lesson with the math teacher, he was struck with how engaged the students had been and how many math concepts they had learned during that class period. He admitted that he was pleasantly surprised by how much they were able to accomplish during the lesson and said that he was going to allow them to use graphing calculators more often.

Pam

EXPECT MORE

Hold high expectations for all students, and avoid deficit views of diverse learners.

Many in the general public and in education attribute the "achievement gap" to cultural deficits in low-income communities of color. There is a belief that non-White communities are not capable of achieving academically, except for the few exceptions who conform to White cultural values. These attitudes are reinforced by the mainstream media, which perpetuate negative stereotypes of people of color and reject alternative viewpoints. These opinions are also prevalent within educational systems.[1]

If teachers do not come from the communities where they work or have not interacted with the people who live in the communities where they work, then the only information they have about these communities is what they receive through the media. A 2017 study from the organization Color of Change examined representations of families by race in local and national media. Among the findings of the study was that the media over-represents the association of Black people with crime and under-represents the connection

---

1   Leslie Fenwick, "Upending Stereotypes about Black Students," *Education Week* 33, no. 7 (2013): 28–32.

between White people and crime, distorting perceptions of who commits crime.[2] These media distortions have a direct impact on the attitudes of non-Black people toward Black people. For example, the National Opinion Research Center regularly conducts surveys of racial attitudes in America. Although racial attitudes have improved over the years, the surveys still find that more than 30 percent of White respondents think Blacks are less hardworking and more than 20 percent of Whites think Blacks are less intelligent.[3] These negative stereotypes about the academic abilities of Black students, English language learners, and others lead teachers to lower their expectations for students from these groups.

WHY HAVING HIGH EXPECTATIONS IS AN EQUITY ISSUE

We should hold high expectations for learning for all students. However, traditionally structured schools privilege the experiences of dominant groups and tend to view ways of learning that differ from the norm as deficient. Teachers with deficit views tend to see students only in terms of what they don't know, rather than recognizing the strengths they have that can be leveraged to help them learn.[4] These deficit views often show up in the language that teachers use when describing students from marginalized groups based on negative stereotypes, lack of prior knowledge, or labels ascribed to them as a result of standardized testing. Deficit language almost always focuses on characteristics of failing students and their families

---

2   Travis Dixon, "A Dangerous Distortion of Our Families: Representation of Families, by Race, in News and Opinion Media," January 2018, https://colorofchange.org /dangerousdistortion/#.

3   Maria Krysan and Sarah Moberg, *Trends in Racial Attitudes* (Urbana: University of Illinois Institute of Government and Public Affairs, 2016), https://igpa.uillinois.edu /programs/racial-attitudes#section-5.

4   Asa Hilliard, "Behavioral Style, Culture, and Teaching and Learning," *Journal of Negro Education* 60, no. 3 (1992): 370–77.

as the sources of academic problems, rather than teachers' practices and school structures. Below are some examples.

Deficit Language	Problem
Calling this parent is a waste of time. They live in a poor neighborhood where they don't value education.	Makes an assumption based on a stereotype that may or may not be true. Views the family as the problem rather than as a potential partner in finding solutions to academic problems.
Those students don't do their homework. They are lazy and don't care about learning.	Makes assumptions about a student's motives for not doing homework that are often influenced by negative stereotypes about marginalized students. Focusing on the student's motivation keeps the teacher from focusing on their behaviors and strategies that can improve student learning, such as examining the quality of assignments, improving the likelihood of success on the assignments, and giving assignments that the students find valuable.
What is wrong with these kids?	Makes assumptions that the problem lies within individual students rather than with the practices, structures, and lack of supports necessary for academic success for these students.

Our ELL and Special Ed students lowered our school's performance last year.	Places the responsibility for the school's performance on the students rather than on the adults responsible for teaching and learning.
	Once again focuses on the children as the problem, rather than the practices, structures, and strategies that can help ELL and Special Ed students be successful.
These kids don't know their basic facts. How am I going to be able to teach them algebra?	Wrongly assumes that all math knowledge is hierarchical, meaning that students can't learn higher-level math until they've mastered all the math topics before.
	This statement most often communicates that the teacher lacks confidence in their own ability to be successful with students with a previous history of low math achievement.
These kids aren't capable of higher-order thinking.	Makes assumptions about what students can or cannot do based on previous history with them.
	Keeps the focus on students' past performance, rather than on teacher practices that can support higher-order thinking for all students.
These are my ____ kids. Fill in the blank with bubble, level 1, low-level, etc.	All students have areas of strength and weakness in mathematics. Identifying students by the labels assigned to them through standardized tests is dehumanizing and reinforces a social hierarchy often influenced by negative stereotypes of marginalized groups.

Teachers will often lower their expectations and "water down" the curriculum because they believe that a certain group of students cannot handle the rigor of critical thinking. For example, well-meaning teachers often differentiate learning for their struggling learners by making problems easier for them. However, this approach often backfires when students are no longer motivated to do the work. According to expectancy value theory, motivation = expectancy × value, indicating that both of these factors must be high in order for students to be motivated to complete academic tasks.[5] Students need to be able to affirmatively answer both of the following questions: (1) Am I likely to be successful at this task? and (2) Do I perceive this task to be valuable? When teachers try to increase students' ability to complete a task by making it easier, unwittingly they undermine student motivation by making the task less valuable. Therefore, it is important to maintain high standards and rigor for struggling students by providing supports that build on students' prior knowledge, number sense, and reasoning skills rather than rely on low-level remedial work. Having high expectations for struggling students is not about giving them more difficult problems; it means identifying what obstacles prevent students from learning and moving them out of the way.

Since the 1920s, standardized testing has been a staple in education as a way to monitor the progress of student learning and to rank and sort students and schools. Critics have long decried the racialized nature of standardized tests. In his research on the history of standardizing testing in the United States, Wayne Au, professor in the School of Educational Studies at the University of Washington, Bothell, explains that standardized tests have been used to prove the

---

5 Allan Wigfield, Jacquelynne S. Eccles, and Stephen M. Tonks, "Expectancy Value Theory in Cross-Cultural Perspective," in *Big Theories Revisited*, ed. Gregory Arief D. Liem and Dennis M. McInerney (Charlotte, VA: Information Age Publishing, 2004), 165–98.

superiority of affluent Whites over the poor and people of color and justify racial inequalities in the larger society.[6]

Test performance gaps also fall along racial lines, with White and Asian students scoring higher than Black and Latinx students. There are a number of reasons for these disparities. Norm referenced tests are designed so that 50 percent of test takers score below the mean. The students most likely to score below the mean are those students who attend schools that are under-resourced and have the least prepared teachers. Doing well on standardized tests requires students to be able to read text, pull out the relevant information, and use that information to solve a problem and come up with the correct solution. Students whose instruction has focused on rote memorization and drill-and-practice are going to be illequipped to meet the expectations for proficient or advanced performance on standardized tests. One result of the testing during the NCLB era was the labeling of students based upon their test scores. Students scored advanced, proficient, basic, below basic, and far below basic. We often hear teachers make statements like, "These are my far-below-basic students." These types of labels further stereotype students, impact how teachers view and treat them, and often result in students being tracked into low-level, skill-based classes.

Once a student has been labeled and placed on a low track, it is virtually impossible for them to move to a higher track. This means that they are less likely to be placed on a college preparatory mathematics track in high school. In addition to that, their post-secondary and career options will be severely limited.

---

6   Wayne Au, "Racial Justice Is Not a Choice: White Supremacy, High Stakes Testing, and the Punishment of Black and Brown students," *Rethinking Schools* 33, no. 4 (Summer 2019): https://rethinkingschools.org/articles/racial-justice-is-not-a-choice/.

WHAT HAPPENS WHEN WE DON'T HAVE HIGH EXPECTATIONS

Patricia's Story

When my Tech Math II classes received their tests back on slope and equations of lines, the results were terrible. Even though we had been going so slowly on this section—it was the only thing we had been doing for the three weeks I'd been at the school—just about everyone failed miserably. The highest score in my third-period class was a 75.

When I handed the tests back, most of the kids were laughing about how poorly they had done. None of them seemed upset about their grades at all. It was very disappointing. For the most part, these students appeared as though they wanted to learn, but they failed to put in the extra effort outside of class. I wondered if maybe they were just so used to not doing well that neither they nor their parents cared anymore. I know if I had brought a grade like that home, there definitely would have been consequences, but I would have bet money after that test that most of my students' parents wouldn't ground them or even say a word about being disappointed in their grades. If they had, I suspected there would be much more effort from my students to do well in class.

To me, these seemed like such basic problems, and I wondered, if my students couldn't get these problems correct, how in the world could they move on to harder ones? But, many of the students proved me wrong and did go on to do better on the harder problems. On the original test, I think they made a lot of careless errors, but when the questions were more challenging, for the most part, they were more careful.

Even new teachers who start out with high expectations often lower them when they begin to see students behaving in ways that align with their biases. Patricia is an educator who began her student teaching semester with high expectations for her students but later adopted deficit views of their motivation and ability when they consistently missed meeting her expectations. Rather than attribute their lack of achievement to her limited repertoire of instructional strategies, she blamed their low achievement on laziness or lack of parental support. Patricia fell into the trap of thinking that students who perform at lower levels are incapable of achieving at higher levels. However, her students ended up proving her wrong as the class moved on to more engaging higher-level material.

Test preparation replaces genuine teaching and learning

One impact of low teacher expectation related to standardized testing has been the overreliance on test preparation as part of the curriculum. During the NCLB era, when schools were rewarded or sanctioned based upon their test scores, low-performing schools and districts responded with scripted curricula and monthly benchmark tests. Teachers were instructed by administrators to focus on "bubble kids," those students who were close to moving from basic to proficient, and ignore the lower-performing students. Valuable instructional time was wasted on test preparation, which usually consisted of a focus on skills and procedures as opposed to problem solving and critical thinking. Often, students were placed in front of computer screens to practice basic skills over and over again.

Tracking

One of the most insidious practices in education today is the tracking or grouping of students by perceived ability. Teachers often use standardized test scores as an excuse for tracking. They feel that low-performing students will hold back high-performing students. Their solution is to group together students they perceive as having the same abilities. At the elementary level, this manifests as high and low groups, where students in high groups are allowed to engage in high-level, cognitively demanding tasks, and students in low groups practice basic skills. At the high school level, students perceived as high performing are placed into a college preparatory mathematics sequence, and students perceived as low performing are placed in classes that do not prepare them for college, like two-year algebra classes or mathematics support classes. Unfortunately, these placements usually fall along racial lines.

A particular problem here arises in algebra placement during the transition from middle school to high school. Placement in algebra at the high school level is very subjective, and many high schools have arbitrary criteria for doing so. A study by the Noyce Foundation of several high schools in Northern California found that 60 percent of students who passed eighth-grade algebra were placed into an algebra course again in high school. The report also found that, although 53 percent of Black students took algebra in eighth grade, only 18 percent were placed into geometry in ninth grade.[7] The situation became so problematic that, in 2015, the state legislature passed the California Mathematics Placement Act, requiring high schools to work with communities to develop objective algebra placement criteria and make the policy accessible for everyone.[8]

Letting Low-Achieving Students Off the Hook

One harmful result that comes from teachers not having high expectations for students is that they often fail to hold students of color responsible for a high level of performance. Because of stereotypes and fears about student resistance, teachers sometimes allow students to disengage from the work of the class if they agree not to be disruptive. This does a disservice to the student, who learns that, if

---

7   Steve Waterman, "Pathways Report: Dead Ends and Wrong Turns on the Path through Algebra," report for the Noyce Foundation, April 4, 2010, https://www.siliconvalleycf .org/sites/default/files/documents/misplacement/Pathways-Report.pdf.

8   "Implementing the California Mathematics Placement Act of 2015," California Department of Education, January 13, 2016, https://www.cde.ca.gov/nr/el/le /yr13ltr0113a.asp.

they can intimidate the teacher, they will not be held accountable. The student also ends up failing the class because they have not done any of the work.

Kyndall once supervised a first-year teacher who was working at an urban middle school. The student population of the school was approximately 90 percent Latinx and 10 percent African American. In this class, there were about thirty students, twenty-eight of them Latinx and two African American, one of whom was female and the other of whom was male. The students sat in groups of four at tables arranged so they could face one another.

On the day Kyndall visited the class, all of the students except one were sitting in groups. Melvin, the African American boy, was instead sitting at what appeared to be the teacher's desk, alone, using a laptop. The lesson plan for the day was to have the students work together in their groups on an investigation. The teacher began the period by explaining to the students what their task was and passing out written instructions to the students. Through all of this, Melvin appeared not to be paying attention to the teacher's instructions.

After getting the students set up for the activity, the teacher circulated around the room to monitor progress, leaving them to work on their own and providing support as needed. At one point in the lesson, the teacher became closely involved with one of the groups.

Near to where Melvin was sitting was a group of Latinx boys who seemed to be struggling with either the lesson or the technology. Melvin left his desk, walked over to the group, helped them all get started on the assignment, and then returned to his seat. The boys stayed engaged with the activity for the remainder of the class, but because the teacher was so involved with the other group, she completely missed what Melvin had done to help them.

When Kyndall asked the teacher why she had Melvin sitting by himself, she replied that Melvin rarely engaged in classwork, and she would rather have him sit alone and do nothing than be disruptive. Because of the teacher's low expectations of Melvin, she had no idea that not only was he capable of doing the work, he knew the information well enough to explain it to the other students.

As Kyndall left the class, he passed by Melvin, looked him in his eyes, and said, "I saw what you did in class today!" Melvin looked up at him, eyes wide, and said, "What are you talking about?" Kyndall just kept walking, feeling good for validating what Melvin had done.

EXPECTING MORE

Teachers with high expectations provide opportunities for all of their students to make sense of problems and persevere in solving them. If students are constantly asked to blindly follow procedures they do not understand, they will eventually come to believe that mathematics is not supposed to make sense. A steady diet of low-level worksheets that place a very low cognitive demand on students produces mathematically anemic students who will never have the opportunity to learn how to persevere or make sense of problems. The types of tasks teachers assign communicate their beliefs about students' abilities more than any words could.

Using assets-based language

Expecting more means viewing students as having funds of knowledge and rich cultural experiences and as coming from communities that use mathematics on a regular basis. Expecting more also requires teachers to be mindful of the language they use to talk about students. Too often, teachers label students' mathematical ability by their standardized test scores. Deficit language is also used as a way to compare Black, Latinx, and poor students to a White or Asian standard.

In the "What Have You Heard?" activity described in chapter 2, participants have an opportunity to practice reframing deficit descriptions of students into assets-based descriptions. Participants are given a list of deficit descriptions of Black boys and mathematics. Participants are then challenged to take each deficit description and reframe it to make it an assets-based description. Examples of deficit descriptions and their reframed assets-based descriptions are listed in the table below.

Deficit Description	Reframed Assets-Based Description
Don't feel they need math; want to be successful at sports	Scholar athletes
Low attention	High energy to learn
Families don't support	Supportive, caring families
Poor math students	Mathematical thinkers
Slow learners	Highly capable
Not motivated/ambitious	Highly motivated

When teachers have an opportunity to practice reframing deficit language to assets-based language, they become a lot more conscious of the language they use to describe the students they work with.

Low-floor, high-ceiling tasks

It is especially important to engage marginalized students in the Standards for Mathematical Practice. Making sense of problems and persevering in solving them, reasoning abstractly and quantitatively, constructing viable arguments and critiquing the reasoning of others, modeling with mathematics, using appropriate tools strategically, attending to precision, looking for and making use of structure, and looking for and expressing regularity in repeated reasoning are the behaviors that will make them smarter in mathematics. All students, regardless of perceived ability, are capable of engaging in high-level, cognitively demanding mathematics tasks. If teachers are willing to look past their preconceived notions and give students opportunities to do mathematics, they might be surprised with what they are able to do.

One instructional strategy to capture the interest of all students is the use of low-floor, high-ceiling tasks. These are tasks that allow all students to participate at whatever level they are and can be extended for enrichment. Growth pattern tasks are one type of low-floor, high-ceiling task (previously mentioned in chapter 5). As long as a student can recognize patterns and count, they can partake in these tasks. When teachers help students see the connection between the different representations for the growth pattern, they are helping students build their mathematical understanding. We have seen students solve growth pattern tasks by extending the pattern visually, creating numerical tables, making coordinate graphs, or writing algebraic equations. We have often witnessed students who were considered low performing come up with more sophisticated representations than students who were perceived to be high performing. These experiences also help to eliminate stereotypes teachers may have about students.

Teachers who have high expectations for their students allow them to do the work of using structure to find the patterns and shortcuts for themselves, rather than doing this work for them. Too many times, teachers feel compelled to provide neatly packaged formulas in order to make it "easier" for their students. Unfortunately, this communicates to students that you do not believe that they are capable of "discovering" the formulas or figuring out how to use them for themselves. Therefore, culturally relevant teachers must reimagine their roles as mathematics educators from telling students how to find answers to helping students figure out how to find answers. This shifts students from being passive recipients of information to active creators of knowledge, which, in turn, results in greater retention and increased mathematics achievement.

Genuine math discourse

Teachers with high expectations also insist that all students attend to precision when explaining and justifying their thinking. Rather than passing judgment on the informal language that students bring with them, culturally relevant teachers use students' informal language as a bridge to help them use more precise academic vocabulary while communicating mathematically.

The only way for teachers to really know what students are thinking and feeling is to engage them in written and oral discourse. Students also benefit from hearing each other's ideas. Journals can be used for students to record their solutions to problems, as a place to do the daily warm-up exercise or exit slip, or as a venue to share their feelings about the class or their lives. Teachers can use journals to enter into a dialogue with their students in ways that build positive relationships.

There are a variety of methods to help students participate in oral discourse. A popular activity is "Think-Pair-Share." Students are given a task to solve and then take a few minutes to work on it by themselves. Next, students pair up with a classmate to share their thinking. If students are working in groups, the conversation can be expanded to include four or more students sharing their ideas. As a teacher circulates around the room, they are able to hear what students are thinking and can use this insight to help further the mathematical understanding of the entire class or, if necessary, to correct misconceptions.

Another popular strategy is "Math Talks." First, students are given a problem to solve mentally. This will look different at various grade levels. For instance, an elementary student may be given a subtraction or multiplication problem to solve, whereas an algebra student may be given a linear equation. Students then share their solution strategies verbally. "Math Talks" help children build mental math and computation strategies.[9] When teachers are able to hear the mathematical thinking of their students, they are able to recognize the assets that the students bring to the classroom and build on them more effectively.

Differentiation using parallel and open-ended tasks

Oftentimes, teachers lower the cognitive demand of a task in the name of differentiation. Too many times, well-meaning teachers have interpreted differentiation as providing easier problems for their low-achieving students and harder problems for their high achievers. This practice invariably leads to what is known as the Matthew effect, whereby the most successful students are continually provided the activities that further their success, while low-achieving students are most often deprived of the learning experiences that would improve their academic achievement. The Matthew effect is the educational equivalent of "the rich get richer, and the poor get poorer."[10]

Rather than rescuing students from work by giving them easier problems, teachers will find it more productive to differentiate by using parallel and/or open-ended tasks. In her book, *Good Questions: Great Ways to Differentiate Mathematics Instruction*, Marian Small describes parallel tasks as two or more tasks that allow students at a variety of levels to engage with the big ideas of the lesson.[11] For example, if the standard requires that students understand the effects

9   Sherry Parrish and Jamie Ann Cross, *Number Talks: Helping Children Build Mental Math and Computation Strategies, Grades K–5* (Sausalito, CA: Math Solutions, 2014).

10 Mark Chubb, "Minimizing the 'Matthew Effect,'" *Thinking Mathematically* (blog), January 15, 2018, https://buildingmathematicians.wordpress.com/2018/01/15/minimizing -the-matthew-effect/#:~:text=The%20idea%20of%20the%20Matthew,disadvantage %20continue%20to%20lose%20ground.

11 Marian Small, *Good Questions: Great Ways to Differentiate Mathematics Instruction*, 4th ed. (New York: Teachers College Press, 2020).

of changing various numbers in an absolute value equation, one task might require students to graph the parent graph y = |x| by hand and then compare various absolute value graphs with their equations to generalize the principle. A parallel task would provide a graph of the parent graph, and then give students a graphing calculator to generalize the transformation principles. Both tasks require students to generalize the principles. A task that gave students the generalization in the form of a rule or procedure and only asked them to apply it would not be parallel, but rather a watered-down version of the task.

Instead of providing two or more different tasks, teachers can also differentiate mathematics instruction by providing all students the same open-ended question that is rich enough to evoke a broad range of responses at many levels. Applying the strategy of reversibility to traditional math problems can produce open-ended questions that can give students with varying abilities access to the same math content. Rather than asking students the answer to 23 + 14, teachers can ask them to create questions where the answer is 37. The strategy of variability can create open-ended questions like, "Make this sentence true in as many ways as you can: ____% of _____ is 23." Asking how things are alike and different can also create open-ended questions like, "¾ and ⅔: If I asked you how these numbers were alike and different, what would you suggest?"

Be a warm demander

Lisa Delpit describes culturally relevant teachers as "warm demanders" who hold students accountable for high academic achievement, while at the same time providing them the social support they need to succeed. These warm demanders apply the strategy of Academic Press, which means making the content clear, holding high expectations for students, and providing the necessary assistance for students to be successful. Warm demanders also develop strong social relationships, build trust and confidence in their students, and provide psychological safety that allows for taking risks, admitting errors, asking for help, and experiencing failure.

Warm demanders do not allow low-achieving students to opt out of doing cognitively demanding work. They provide support for their students without doing all of the thinking for them. We use the analogy that a warm demander acts more like a compass than a GPS. Even though a GPS gives very specific step-by-step directions to a desired location, most students can recall a time when a GPS was wrong and led them astray. This is why it is important to provide guidance to students in ways that do not sacrifice long-term understanding for short-term test results. "Don't GPS me!" became a common phrase among Pam's students. What this meant was that they needed help with math in ways that would allow them to understand the process. They knew the power of true understanding and the pitfalls of following directions they did not comprehend. There is a GEICO commercial on YouTube called The Great Penguin Migration that illustrates this point, when, after receiving faulty information from the GPS, the penguin searching for the breeding ground says, "Nope, nope! I'm going to follow my instincts!"

Warm demanders also engage in strategies that require all students to be actively engaged. One way to do this is by randomly calling on all students, not just volunteers. This routine communicates to all students that they are capable and accountable for learning. When teachers randomly place students in groups on a regular basis, they communicate high expectations for learning. Peter Liljedahl, professor of mathematics education in the Faculty of Education and an associate member in the Department of Mathematics at Simon Fraser University in Canada, has performed research that suggests that, when teachers visibly randomize student groups on a frequent basis, there is an increase of knowledge shared between students, a decrease in reliance on the teacher for answers, and an increase in both enthusiasm for mathematics class and engagement in mathematics tasks.[12]

You may be thinking that you do have high expectations for your students, but there are some students who consistently fail to meet those expectations. You may be thinking about students like Jasmine, who actively oppose your attempts to help them learn through defiance or passively do so by not participating in class and failing to complete assignments. Since negative stereotypes impact students in a variety of ways, the effects of your efforts may take time. Having high expectations for all students requires us to believe in the humanity of our students and their ability to grow and change. When Pam reached out to Myra to shake her hand before class, she had no way of knowing whether it would change anything. Up to that point, all of Pam's attempts to engage Myra were met with a cold silence. However, shaking Myra's hand did make a difference, and Pam would have never known that had she not kept trying. Similarly, Pam did not know that the Georgia Milestones project would have such an impact on Jasmine. The reality is that it will take some students longer to respond to our efforts than others, and that's okay. Because marginalized students are often impacted by negative stereotypes in ways that we may not totally understand, having high expectations for students from marginalized groups compels us to keep trying to meaningfully engage them in the teaching and learning process.

---

12 Peter Liljedahl, "The Affordances of Using Visually Random Groups in a Mathematics Classroom," in *Transforming Mathematics Instruction: Multiple Approaches and Practices*, ed. Yeping Li, Ed Silver, and Shiqi Li (New York: Springer, 2014).

— QUESTIONS TO CONSIDER —

1. Which of your behaviors communicate low expectations to students?
2. What causes you to "rescue" students prematurely by giving them the answers or telling them what to do?
3. How can you make sure you do not lower the cognitive demand on your students when they struggle?

— CALL TO ACTION —

1. List the two ideas you learned from this chapter that are most relevant to your practice.
2. Complete the action plan below for each idea.

Idea 1:	
Vision for your students if you implement this idea in your classroom, school, or district	
Action step	
Deadline for action step	
Person you will ask to hold you accountable for completing this action step	

Idea 2:	
Vision for your students if you implement this idea in your classroom, school, or district	
Action step	
Deadline for action step	
Person you will ask to hold you accountable for completing this action step	

CONCLUSION

It is our belief that many of the principles in the ICUCARE framework overlap, and many of the strategies introduced in one chapter are applicable in other chapters. It is hard to release control if you don't have high expectations for your students. It is difficult to assess, activate, and build on prior knowledge if you don't understand your students well.

We encourage you to use our book as part of a book study or in a professional learning community. Our suggestion is to study one chapter at a time. Choose a partner and try some of the activities out in your classrooms. Share student work. Share successes and challenges with each other. If something doesn't work the first time, don't give up. Use the questions provided at the end of each chapter to reflect on your work. Use the call to action to set goals and hold yourself accountable.

We have given you a variety of tools to begin to make your classroom a more equitable space for all students. The work of sharing our journey is done; it is now your responsibility to use the resources in this book. An ICUCARE Checklist has been included in Appendix D to help you keep track of resources and strategies you have tried from this book. Will you join us on this journey?

For every reason we can give about why marginalized students don't do well in math (e.g., poverty, unsupportive families, fear of math), we should use these as the same reasons why we must do better. Students in poverty must become math literate to escape poverty. Students must be able to rely on teachers to support their success in mathematics when they don't have that support at home. Only a math teacher can bring healing for students who have been traumatized by past math experiences. At the end of the day, it's not about which strategies we are comfortable with using, it's whether or not we are comfortable with the level of our students' learning.

It is our hope that reading this book has been like taking off blinders, helping you to get a better glimpse of your students, yourself, and the structures in which both of you exist. By making the choice to see the impact of negative stereotypes on marginalized students, you also are able to see an inequitable system that privileges those who are White and middle class at the expense of other students. We are grateful you chose to learn with us as we seek answers for the problems that keep many students from taking full advantage of their education, knowing that we cannot find these answers alone.

We do not believe that our efforts alone are sufficient for solving the problem of poor mathematical achievement among diverse learners. We do not believe that our vision—or any vision—will ever be perfect or that our interpretations will not have to be adjusted. As soon as our vision becomes focused, the landscape will likely change, and we will no longer be looking at the same vista. We do, however, believe that our vision of equity mathematics instruction is clearer now than when we began writing this book. Our hope is that others reading it will see more clearly after taking off the blinders in the mathematics classroom that privilege the culture of White, middle-class students while ignoring the role that other cultures play in the learning process. While reading this book may have raised even more questions than it has answered, we are convinced that this process of discovery and insight will be worth the effort when you stand in the power of knowing you are an advocate for marginalized students each and every day.

APPENDIX A:
FIND SOMEONE WHO ACTIVITY

Find someone in the classroom who knows how to solve a problem below and have them explain it to you. Once they have explained it so that you understand it, have them sign their name to the problem. Then find someone else who can explain another problem. Continue this process until all problems have been completed.

Find the sum of twenty-three and thirty-two.	Find the difference of seven tenths and three hundredths.	Find the product of one fourth and three eighths.
Find the quotient of sixty-seven and eleven.	FREE SPACE	Write the prime factorization of seventy-two.
Find forty percent of eighty dollars.	Draw an obtuse triangle.	Write a polynomial with a degree of two.

Appendix B:
Groupworthy Task
Checklist

1. Seeing visual patterns
2. Asking questions of the group to get all ideas out on the table
3. Representing situations using mathematical symbols
4. Organizing information
5. Making connections between different methods
6. Developing convincing arguments about the correctness of a solution

Name	Ability 1	Ability 2	Ability 3	Ability 4	Ability 5	Ability 6
Algernon						
Brittany						
Caleb						
David						
Evan						
Faith						
Gavin						
Hailey						
Inez						
Javier						
Kyle						

Lisa						
Mary						
Nicholas						
Odessa						
Patricia						
Quiana						
Rita						
Steven						
Travis						
Ulysses						
Valerie						
Winona						
Xavier						
Yasmin						
Zachary						

APPENDIX C:
CULTURALLY RELEVANT
MODIFIED TASKS

Below I describe the process that I used to take a standards-aligned task and turn it into a culturally relevant task.

ELEMENTARY SCHOOL EXAMPLE

Standard 3.OA.8 Solve two-step word problems using the four operations. Represent these problems using equations with a letter standing for the unknown quantity. Assess the reasonableness of answers using mental computation and estimation strategies, including rounding.

Learning Target: I can use all four operations to solve two-step word problems.

Original Task:

There were 56 birdhouses at school. Today, 4 classes made more birdhouses. Each class made 8 birdhouses. How many total birdhouses are there now?

Source:

Student Achievement Partners. "Two-Step Problems Using the Four Operations Mini-assessment." *Achieve the Core.* Last modified November 7, 2019. https://achievethecore.org/page/2782/two -step-problems-using-the-four-operations-mini-assessment.

Context for Modification:

Modifying tasks to make them culturally relevant begins with the principle *Understand Your Students Well*. As a result of this principle, the following observations were made. This task was modified for a third-grade math class in the metropolitan Atlanta area. The class was 83 percent African American, 5 percent White, 7 percent Hispanic, 54 percent female, and 100 percent economically disadvantaged. The teacher noticed several students showed interest in the civil rights movement and had read books about Rosa Parks and Dr. Martin Luther King Jr. Other students had expressed a desire to have their own businesses when they became adults. Because Black females were prominently featured in the text of the modified task, this activity could operate as a mirror for the Black female students in the class and as a window for the rest of the students.

Hints for Implementation:

Teachers can do a Think-Pair-Share to assess the prior knowledge of the Montgomery Bus Boycott. The video that accompanies the task tells the story of the Montgomery Bus Boycott. Prior to showing the video, teachers can pose questions for students to think about as they watch the video. The questions should have students determine the reasons for the boycott, how African Americans were able to sustain the boycott, and the role that the taxis played in supporting the boycott. After the students have seen the video, they can respond to the reflection questions verbally and/or in writing in small groups prior to a whole class discussion.

Modified Task:

There were many women who took part in the movement for civil rights for African Americans. While most people are familiar with how Rosa Parks refused to give up her seat on a bus in Montgomery, Alabama, on December 1, 1955, very few people know that a fifteen-year-old African American girl named Claudette Colvin refused to give up her seat nine months earlier. Because of their treatment on the buses, the African American residents of Montgomery organized a boycott, meaning they refused to ride the buses, until they could sit wherever they wanted to. Therefore, they had to find other methods of transportation to and from work. This provided an opportunity for African American taxi drivers to transport boycotters as an alternative to the buses.

Let's say during the boycott, the taxi driver charged 8 cents per passenger. The first hour the driver worked, he made 56 cents. For the second hour, the taxi driver transported 4 people. How much total money did the taxi driver make in the first two hours of work?

Sources:

Adler, Margot, and Phillip Hoose. "Before Rosa Parks, There Was Claudette Colvin." NPR. March 15, 2009. https://www.npr. org/2009/03/15/101719889/before-rosa-parks-there-was -claudette-colvin.

Biography Channel. Montgomery Bus Boycott |American Freedom Stories | Biography. YouTube video, 3:51. January 19, 2014. https://www.youtube.com/watch?v=FE6Yvy—5aw.

Williams, Juan. *Eyes on the Prize: America's Civil Rights Years, 1954–1965.* New York: Penguin Books, 2013.

Solution:

Quantity	Units	Description	Expression
15	years	Age of Claudette Colvin when she refused to give up her seat	Extraneous Information
9	months	Amount of time before Rosa Parks gave up her seat	Extraneous Information

56	cents	Amount of money made during the first hour	56
4	people	Number of people transported in the second hour	4
8	cents	The cost charged for a taxi ride	8
?	cents	Amount earned for the entire day	56 + S
?	cents	Amount earned in the second hour	S = 8 × 4

$\underline{P}$lan/$\underline{S}$olve—Use the relationships between the quantities to write and solve an equation.

$L = 8 \times 4 = 32$

$56 + L = 56 + 32 = 88$

$\underline{C}$heck—Write your answer in a complete sentence, and check to see if your answer is reasonable in the context of the problem.

The taxi driver earned a total of 88 cents the first two hours of work.

Check: $88 - 32 = 56$ (which is how much he started with)

MIDDLE SCHOOL EXAMPLE

Standard 7.RP.3 Use proportional relationships to solve multistep ratio and percent problems. Examples: simple interest, tax, markups and markdowns, gratuities and commissions, and fees.

Learning Target: I can use proportional relationships to solve percent markup and markdown problems.

Original Task:

The selling price of a house dropped from $250,000 to $210,000 over a period of 5 years.

Part A: By what percent did the selling price decrease? (Explain.)

Part B: By what percent does the price need to increase in order to return to its original value of $250,000? (Explain.)

Source:

Brainly User. "The Selling Price of a House." *Brainly.* October 17, 2016. https://brainly.com/question/2003636.

Context for Modification:

This task was modified for a seventh-grade math class in the metropolitan Atlanta area. The following observations supported the *Understand Your Students Well* principle. The class was 40 percent African American, 46 percent White, 10 percent Hispanic, 48 percent female, and 65 percent economically disadvantaged. The teacher noticed the California wildfires had been very prominent in the news, with several students mentioning their concern for residents who had lost their homes. Several thunderstorms had recently come through causing major property damage to houses in the area. Some students had casually referenced that they had family in Louisiana. This task could operate as a window by giving students insight into ways that natural disasters can negatively impact communities that were not directly hit.

Hints for Implementation:

Start the lesson by checking for prior knowledge with a Think-Pair-Share in response to the prompt, "How does a natural disaster affect the price of houses?" Have a whole class discussion about the prompt. Have students work in groups using a literacy strategy to make sense of the text in the article about the impact of wildfires on California real estate (https://www.multihousingnews.com/post/wildfires-impact-on-california-real-estate/). Have the reporter from each group share what they learned about the impact of wildfires on real estate.

Modified Task:

Natural disasters like the wildfires in California or the hurricanes happening in the Southeast not only have negative impacts on the environment but can also cause nearby properties to lose value. For example, the value of a home in Louisiana dropped from $250,000 to $210,000 five years after Hurricane Katrina.

a) By what percentage did the value of the home decrease? Explain how you found your answer.

b) By what percentage does the home value need to increase in order to return to its original value of $250,000? Explain how you found your answer.

Source:

Loria, Keith. "Wildfire's Impact on California Housing." *Multi-Housing News*. November 14, 2018. https://www.multihousingnews.com/post/wildfires-impact-on-california-real-estate/.

Solution:

Quantity	Units	Description	Expression
250,000	$	Original value of the home	O
210,000	$	Reduced value of the home	R
5	years	Time period the value dropped	Extraneous Information

?	%	% of value decrease	$[(O-R)/O] \times 100$
?	%	% increase needed to restore home to original value	$[(O-R)/R] \times 100$

Visual model for part A

100% = $250,000 = O

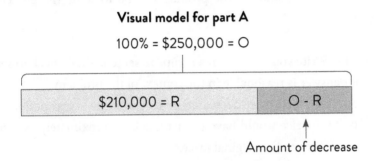

Amount of decrease

Visual model for part B

100%

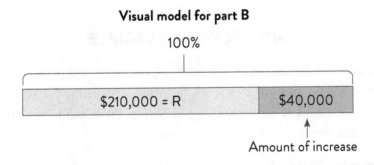

Amount of increase

<u>Plan</u>/<u>Solve</u>—Use the relationships between the quantities to write and solve an equation.

Part A:

$$[(O - R)/O] \times 100 = [(250{,}000 - 210{,}000)/250{,}000] \times 100 = 16$$

Explanation: I subtracted the reduced value from the original value and divided the difference by the original value. Then I multiplied the decimal product by 100 to write the percent decrease.

Part B:

$$[(O - R)/R] \times 100 = [(250{,}000 - 210{,}000)/210{,}000] \times 100 =$$
$$19.047619\% \approx 19\%$$

Explanation: I divided the difference in the two values by the reduced value. Then I multiplied the product by 100 to write the percent increase.

<u>C</u>heck—Write your answer in a complete sentence and check to see if your answer is reasonable in the context of the problem.

    a. The house price decreased by 16% over the 5-year period.

    b. The price would have to increase by approximately 19% to return to the original price.

Check: $210{,}000 \times 1.19047619 = \$250{,}000$ √

HIGH SCHOOL EXAMPLE

Standard A.REI.4b Solve quadratic equations by inspection (e.g., for $x^2 = 49$), taking square roots, factoring, completing the square, and the quadratic formula, as appropriate to the initial form of the equation (limit to real number solutions).

Learning Target: I can solve quadratic equation factoring, completing the square, using the quadratic formula, or using graphing technology.

Original Task:

Solve the following equations:

    a. $16x^2 + 10x - 27 = -6x + 5$

    b. $2x^2 + 32x + 90 = 0$

Context for Modification:

This task was modified for a high school algebra I class in the metropolitan Atlanta area. Pam implemented the *Understand Your
Students Well* principle by making the following observations. The
class was 100 percent African American, 50 percent female, and 60
percent economically disadvantaged. A large number of students had
seen the *Hidden Figures* movie. Many organizations within the community (e.g., schools, clubs, churches, fraternal organizations) had
sponsored trips for young people to see the movie at local theaters.
Local newspapers and radio and television stations featured stories
about the characters and actors in the movie. Many students were
familiar with the actress Taraji P. Henson from the *Empire* television
show and the actress Janelle Monáe, a popular hip-hop recording
artist. Pam felt that all of these features would make *Hidden Figures*
a great context that would be engaging and relevant for her students.
Because students could see people who looked like them reflected in
the text, this task would operate as a mirror for Pam's students.

Hints for Implementation:

The videos that accompany the lesson provide information about
the Smithsonian National Museum of African American History
and Culture and tell the stories of the three main characters in the
Hidden Figures movie. The videos can be used in a variety of ways
to support the lesson. Teachers can have students watch all of the
videos at once before solving the problems, or they can have the students watch the video about Mary Jackson prior to part A and the
video about Dorothy Vaughan before part B. It is up to the teacher
to decide what makes the best sense for their instructional goals.
Prior to viewing the videos, the teacher should create some questions for the students to think about as they watch the stories. After
the students have seen the movies, they can respond to the reflection

questions verbally and/or in writing in small groups prior to a whole class discussion.

Modified Task:

The movie *Hidden Figures* tells the story of how three African American women, Katherine Johnson, Dorothy Vaughan, and Mary Jackson, teamed up to solve NASA's mathematical equations during the space race in the sixties. Some papers have been discovered at NASA that include graphs, tables, and calculations that may have belonged to these ladies. Your job is to organize these papers into a collection that can be displayed at the Smithsonian National Museum of African American History and Culture in Washington, DC. You may review the following websites to familiarize yourself with this work.

- https://nmaahc.si.edu/
- https://www.youtube.com/watch?v=egYTxxKylv8
- https://www.youtube.com/watch?v=nKxgieXQ82w
- https://www.youtube.com/watch?v=ovcbmwQPTq0
- https://www.youtube.com/watch?v=GeM-Pb0xtEk

Part A

You come across another document with the following function, $16x^2 + 10x - 27 = -6x + 5$, and wonder if it might have belonged to Janelle Monáe, I mean Mary Jackson. Based on a previous interview, Ms. Jackson recalled that she was missing a document with an equation that had 3 as one of its solutions. Could this document be Ms. Jackson's missing document? Explain your reasoning and show work to support your answer.

Part B

One of Dorothy Vaughan's roles was to double-check the work of the "computers" she supervised. The work of one of her "computers" solved an equation as shown below.

$2x^2 + 32x + 90 = 0$

$\rightarrow \dfrac{2x^2}{2} + \dfrac{32x}{2} + \dfrac{90}{2} = \dfrac{0}{2}$

$\rightarrow x^2 + 16x + \dfrac{45}{-45} = \dfrac{0}{-45}$

$\rightarrow x^2 + 16x = -45$

$\rightarrow x^2 + 16x + 8 = -45 + 8$

$\rightarrow (x + 8)2 = -37$

$\rightarrow x + 8 = -37$

$\rightarrow x = -37 - 8$

$\rightarrow x = -45$

What mistakes did the "computer" make? Explain your reasoning.

Part C

Before any document can be included in the collection at the Smithsonian National Museum of African American History and Culture, it must be worked correctly. Rework the problem above to find the correct solution(s). Show work to support your answer.

Sources:

ABC News. "NASA Headquarters Renamed for 'Hidden Figure' | WNT." YouTube video, 1:55. June 24, 2020. https://.youtube .com/watch?v=GeM-Pb0xtEk.

CBS This Morning. "The African-American Women behind NASA's Rocket Launches." YouTube video, 5:04. September 7, 2016. https://www.youtube.com/watch?v=egYTxxKylv8.

Gal's Guide to the Galaxy. "Your Gal, Dorothy Vaughan." YouTube video, 1:52. February 9, 2018. https://youtube.com/watch ?v=ovcbmwQPTq0.

NASA Television. "Katherine Johnson: An American Hero." YouTube video, 2:05. February 24, 2020. https://youtube.com /watch?v=nKxgieXQ82w.

National Museum of African American History and Culture. https://nmaahc.si.edu.

Solution:

Part A

- Correct answer: No, the document could NOT be Ms. Jackson's missing document.
- Possible explanation to support answer: The correct solutions are -2 and -1. 3 is NOT one of these solutions.
- Possible work that supports the correct answer:

$$16x^2 + 10x - 27 = -6x + 5$$

$$\rightarrow \frac{16x^2}{16} + \frac{16x}{16} - \frac{32}{16} = 0$$

$$\rightarrow x^2 + x - 2 = 0$$

$$\rightarrow (x + 2)(x + 1) = 0 \text{ zero product property}$$

$$\rightarrow x + 2 = 0 \text{ or } x + 1 = 0$$

$$\rightarrow x = -2 \text{ or } x = -1$$

Part B

- Mistakes:
    - She failed to square 8 before adding it to both sides.
    - She also forgot to take the square root of both sides of $(x + 8)^2 = -37$.

Part C

- Correctly worked problem:

$$2x^2 + 32x + 90 = 0$$

$$\rightarrow \frac{2x^2}{2} + \frac{32x}{2} + \frac{90}{2} = \frac{0}{2}$$

$\rightarrow x^2 + 16x + \underline{45} = \underline{0}$
$ -45 \quad -45$

$\rightarrow x^2 + 16x = -45$

$\rightarrow x^2 + 16x + 64 = -45 + 64$

$\rightarrow (x + 8)^2 = 19$

$\rightarrow x + \underline{8} = \underline{19}$
$ -8 \quad -8$

- Correct solutions:

  $x = -8 \; 19$

APPENDIX D:
ICUCARE CHECKLIST

Principle	Actions
Include others as experts	
Be Critically conscious	
Understand your students	
Use Culturally relevant curricula	
Assess, activate, and build on prior knowledge	
Release control	
Expect more	

APPENDIX E:
COMMUNICATION STYLES ACTIVITY

Hawk, Rabbit, Tiger, Turtle: Focusing on Communication Styles

Purpose: A light activity intended to clarify different styles of communication, propose methods of communicating with those whose styles are different from yours, and share ideas on how to value all styles of communication.

Materials and Resources:
- Activity Protocol
- Post-it Chart Paper
- Thick Markers

Preparation and Setup:
- Four sets of charts are needed for this activity.

Chart Set I: 4 charts (1 per group)
1. Make one chart for each of the four animals (hawk, tiger, rabbit, and turtle).
2. Post animal signs at four corners of the room, so that the distance between each group is great enough that discussion within each group is not disturbed by the other groups' discussion and the distance between each group is small enough that when people share, others can hear the group's report.

Activity courtesy of UCLA Teacher Education Program.(2001). "Hawk, Rabbit, Turtle, Tiger: Focusing on Communication Styles."

3. Each group lists the characteristics of the communication style for the animal they chose.

| Hawk | Rabbit | Tiger | Turtle |

Chart Set II: 12 charts (3 per group)

1. Make three charts for each animal group, asking one question on each chart:

   - *How do we feel or what do we think about the other three styles of communication?*
   - *How is each style different from ours?*
   - *How does each style present a challenge to us? Why?*

For example, Hawk group charts should look like this:

Hawk	Hawk	Hawk
How do we feel or what do we think about the other three styles of communication? Rabbit: Tiger: Turtle:	How is each style different from ours? Rabbit: Tiger: Turtle:	How does each style present a challenge to us? Why? Rabbit: Tiger: Turtle:

Chart Set III: 4 charts (1 per group)

1. Make one chart for each animal group, asking the following question:

   - *In what ways can we work to effectively communicate with the _____?*

The charts should look like this:

Hawk	Rabbit
In what ways can we work to effectively communicate with the _____?	In what ways can we work to effectively communicate with the _____?
Rabbit:	Turtle:
Turtle:	Tiger:
Tiger:	Hawk:

Tiger	Turtle
In what ways can we work to effectively communicate with the _____?	In what ways can we work to effectively communicate with the _____?
Turtle:	Hawk:
Hawk:	Rabbit:
Rabbit:	Tiger:

Chart Set IV: 4 charts (1 per group)

1. Make one chart for each group, asking the following question:
   - *What do those with differing styles of communication need to know about communication with us?*

The charts should look like this:

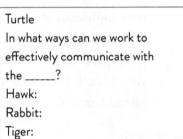

Hawk	Rabbit
What do those with differing styles of communication need to know about communicating with us?	What do those with differing styles of communication need to know about communicating with us?

Tiger	Turtle
What do those with differing styles of communication need to know about communicating with us?	What do those with differing styles of communication need to know about communicating with us?

Process:

Introduction

- Introduce the purpose of the activity.
- Post Chart I at four corners of the room and introduce the four animals.
- Ask students to silently reflect on each of the animals, their images, personalities, and styles of communication.
- Ask students to pick the animal that best describes their own individual style of communication. They must select one animal. Explain to the students that this activity is not about personalities, but styles of communication.
- Ask students to move to the corner of the room where their selected animal is posted.

Report Out

Part I—Group Identity

- Ask each group to select a recorder and a presenter.
- Facilitators then ask each person to share his or her reasons for selecting the animal, with their small group.
  - Facilitators should model the activity by sharing his/her own reasons.
  - Each person should have an opportunity to share.
- The recorder from each group should chart responses on the chart paper labeled with their group name.

Report Out

Part II—Looking at the Styles of Others

- Distribute and post Chart Set II to each of the groups.
- Ask students to reflect on the differing styles of communication within each group.
- After listening to how the others have defined their style of communication, ask students to reflect on the differences in communication styles.
- The recorder from each group should chart responses to the three questions for each of the other groups:

○ How do we feel or what do we think about the other three styles of communication?

○ How is each style different from ours?

○ How does each style present a challenge to us? Why?

Report Out

Parts III and IV—Effective Communication

- Distribute and post Chart Set III and Chart Set IV.

- Ask students to discuss what their group can do to communicate with members of the other animal groups and how others can communicate more effectively with them.

- Chart the groups' response to the questions:

  ○ In what ways can we work to effectively communicate with the _____?

  ○ What do those with differing styles of communication need to know about communication with us?

Report Out

Part V—Reflection

- Ask students to silently reflect on how their own communication style and their perceptions of other styles can affect communication.

- Ask students to brainstorm a few "ground rules" for ensuring effective communication dialogue.

- Save their ideas to revisit during their novice year.

Part VI—Debriefing (whole group activity)

- Ask students to respond to the following: One thing I discovered/rediscovered about my communication style is

  _____.

- Remind students that during the course of their novice year, they will be engaged in dialogue/discussion around issues that are sometimes difficult to discuss and/or highly charged. They should revisit what they learned about themselves and others during today's activities to make those discussions productive and meaningful.

APPENDIX F:
ADDITIONAL RESOURCES

Chapter 1: Include Others as Experts

"Jigsaw," The Teacher Toolkit, http://www.theteachertoolkit.com
/index.php/tool/jigsaw.

"Teach Malleable Intelligence," Teach for America,
https://empathiceducation.files.wordpress.com/2011/07/i-1
_teach_malleable_intelligence.pdf.

"Two Minutes Talks," Stokes County Schools Strategies for Student
Engagement, https://sites.google.com/site/stokestechnology
/Home/instructional-strategies-for-engaging-learners
/activating-strategies/two-minute-talks.

"Walk Around Survey," Stokes County Schools Strategies for
Student Engagement, https://sites.google.com/site
/stokestechnology/Home/instructional-strategies-for
-engaging-learners/activating-strategies/walk-around-survey.

Chapter 2: Be Critically Conscious

"Assigning Competence." University of Vermont. http://www.uvm
.edu/~crathbon/188competencetransc.html.

Dweck, Carol. "How to Help Every Child Fulfil Their Potential."
YouTube video, 21:20. September 18, 2013. https://.youtube
.com/watch?v=PVhUdhZxbGI.

Fenwick, Leslie T. "Upending Stereotypes about Black Students."
Education Week. October 9, 2013. https://www.edweek.org
/leadership/opinion-upending-stereotypes-about-black
-students/2013/10.

Fournier, Eric. "Reducing Stereotype Threat." Washington University in St. Louis Center for Teaching and Learning. https://ctl.wustl.edu/resources/reducing-stereotype-threat/. "Stereotype Threat—Psychology in Action." YouTube video, 3:07. September 28, 2009. https://www.youtube.com/watch?v =nGEUVM6QuMg.

Tatum, Beverly Daniel. "Color Blind or Color Conscious: How Schools Acknowledge Racial and Ethnic Identities Will Affect All Students' Educational Experiences." The School Superintendents Association. https://www.aasa.org/School AdministratorArticle.aspx?id=14892.

"Wise Critiques Help Students Succeed." Stanford SPARQ. https://sparq.stanford.edu/solutionswise-critiques-help -students-succeed.

Chapter 3: Understand Your Students Well

The movie *Freedom Writers* tells the story of how Erin Gruwell, a White, suburban woman, was able to connect with her inner-city students in Long Beach, California, by getting to know them, their families, and their neighborhoods. http://www.chasingthefrog.com/reelfaces/freedomwriters.php.

Ball, Tamika N. "Public Stories of Mathematics Educators: I Am From." *Journal of Urban Mathematics Education* 5, no. 2 (2012): 53–54. https://drive.google.com/file/d/1cM vH6pbS8Xtk1o8m42CxvCjNmA_-D5l6/view.

Manning, Chandra. "Know Your Students: Things to Do to Create Positive Relationships at the Beginning of a School Year/ Semester." http://www.livebinders.com/play/play?id=475167 #anchor.

"Making Connections to Motivate Student Learning. Teaching Channel video. https://learn.teachingchannel.com/video /student-motivation-techniques.

"Math in Everyday Life." Teaching Channel video. https://learn
.teachingchannel.com/video/math-for-everyday-life.

"Personality Bingo." http://www.livebinders.com/media/get
/Mza4ODUxNQ==.

"Social Identity Wheel." LSA Inclusive Teaching, University of
Michigan. https://sites.lsa.umich.edu/inclusive-teaching
/sample-activities/social-identity-wheel/.

"Student Interest Inventory." https://www.mcas.k12.in.us/cms/lib5
/IN01001792/Centricity/Domain/86/Curriculum%20Home
/PLP/STUDENTINTERESTINVENTORY.pdf.

What Kids Can Do, Inc. "First Ask, Then Listen: How to Get
Your Students to Help You Teach Them Better: A Teachers
Guide." https://www.schoolreforminitiative.org/download
/first-ask-then-listen-how-to-get-your-students-to-help
-you-teach-them-better-a-teachers-guide/.

Chapter 4: Use Culturally Relevant Curricula

Berry, Robert, Basil Conway, Brian Lawler, and John Staley. *High
School Mathematics Lessons to Explore, Understand, and
Respond to Social Injustice*. Thousand Oaks, CA: Corwin, 2020.

Bishop, Rudine Sims. "Mirrors, Windows and Sliding Doors."
YouTube video, 1:33. January 30, 2015. https://youtube.com
/watch?v=_AAu58SNSyc.

Jones, Shelly. "Mathematics Teachers' Use of the Culturally Relevant
Cognitively Demanding Mathematics Task Framework and
Rubric in the Classroom." *NERA Conference Proceedings
2015*. https://researchgate.net/publication
/311541522_Mathematics_Teachers'_Use_of_the_Culturally
_Relevant_Cognitively_Demanding_Mathematics_Task
_Framework_and_Rubric_in_the_Classroom.

Jones, Shelly. *Women Who Count: Honoring African American Women Mathematicians.* Providence, RI: American Mathematical Society, 2019.

Riddle, Larry. Biographies of Women Mathematicians. https://www.agnesscott.edu/lriddle/women/women.htm.

"Using Metaphors in the Content Areas." https://sites.google.com /site/literacymath/literature-strategies/using-metaphors-in-the -content-area.

Williams, Scott W. "Mathematicians of the African Diaspora." http://www.math.buffalo.edu/mad/00.INDEXmad .html.

Yang, K. Wayne. "Social Justice Mathematics." http://radicalmath .org/main.php?id=SocialJusticeMath.

Chapter 5: Assess, Activate, and Build on Prior Knowledge

Blackburn, Barbara. "8 Strategies to Quickly Assess Prior Knowledge." *Middleweb.* December 31, 2017. https://www. middleweb.com/36652/8-strategies-to-quickly-assess-prior -knowledge.

"Checking for Understanding." https://drive.google.com/file/d/13Sn 6IgzI9le3uJMsRDpotR2n4DUhPEsp/view.

"Clipboards: A Tool for Informal Assessment." Teaching Channel video, 1:26. https://vimeo.com/108402172.

Ferlazzo, Larry. "Teaching That Activates and Leverages Background Knowledge Is an Equity Issue." *Education Week Blog.* June 16, 2020. https://drive.google.com/file/d/1r4o8bNM bwBuY282q9OjQnbTCg1F1HoeJ/view.

"Math Password—Vocabulary Game." https://www.dropbox.com/s /l2r4vz4mheptq5k/Math%20Password%20Vocabulary%20 Game.pdf?dl=0.

Chapter 6: Release Control

Alcala, L. "My Favorite No." YouTube video, 3:02. https://youtube
.com/watch?v=uuDjke-p4Co.

Marks, Jeff. "Students' Ownership and Relinquishing Control."
In *Promoting Purposeful Discourse: Teacher Research in
Mathematics Classrooms*. Ed. Beth Herbei Eisenmann and
Herbie Michelle Cirillo. Reston, VA: National Council of
Teachers of Mathematics, 2010.

"Practicing Perseverance with 'Lifelines.'" Teaching Channel
video. https://learn.teachingchannel.com/video/teaching
-technique-group-work.

"Totally 10: Math Quiz." https://docs.google.com/document/d/11Fk
JwS1Be60ckVrgNIc65iG7LYlvgrgNVi9gzAfOihw/edit.

Chapter 7: Expect More

"Active Participation in Math Class." https://drive.google.com/
file/d/13ajyi7-LvXj5ItZs8_KrVQOTO_Lsj4u6/view.

Bondy, Elizabeth, and Dorene D. Ross. "The Teacher as Warm
Demander." *Educational Leadership* 66, no. 1 (2008):
54–58. https://www.sjsu.edu/faculty/marachi/mle/Warm%20
Demander%20Article.pdf.

Capizzi, Carla. "Are Educators Showing a 'Positive Bias' to Minority
Students?" *Science Daily*. May 4, 2012. https://sciencedaily
.com/releases/2012/05/120504143023.htm.

"Developing a Passion for Math." Teaching Channel video.
https://learn.teachingchannel.com/video/passion-for-math.

Gerstein, Jackie. "Approaching Marginalized Populations from
an Asset Rather Than a Deficit Model of Education." *User
Generated Education* (blog). May 8, 2016.
https://usergeneratededucation.wordpress.com/2016/05/08/
approaching-marginalized-populations-from-an-asset-rather
-than-a-deficit-model/.

Ledlow, Susan. "Roles and Gambits." https://www.dropbox.com/s/ ls8eosxph26kao9/Roles%20and%20Gambits.pdf?dl=0.

Lombardi, Janice D. "The Deficit Model Is Harming Your Students." *Edutopia.* June 14, 2016. https://www.edutopia.org/blog/ deficit-model-is-harming-students-janice-lombardi.

"Math-Talk Learning Community Rubric." https://drive.google. com/file/d/19ZyzJtEEeLEoaz-ZCy0CgfYehuB2CTop/view.

Petty, Geoff. "Feedback: Medals and Missions." http://geoffpetty. com/for-teachers/feedback-and-questions/.

"Stereotype Examples: 5 Common Types." *Your Dictionary.* https:// examples.yourdictionary.com/stereotype-examples.html.

"Talk Moves." https://drive.google.com/ file/d/12X9nP7Tt_wcDa2PchzUDQmxiBGU1AKxP/view.

ACKNOWLEDGMENTS

First, I'd like to acknowledge God's hand in every struggle and success that led me to the completion of this book. I don't believe that it was an accident that I found a kindred spirit in Kyndall when I attended his session on math equity at the NCSM conference in Boston. Thank you, Kyndall, for asking me to join you as a co-author on this book. It has truly been a pleasure writing, discussing, and even sometimes arguing with you while completing this project. I want to thank my husband, Stephen, for his never-ending support of me throughout this process. He truly was the wind beneath my wings while I completed my doctoral program with four young children and worked on this book ten years later. I want to thank my children, Candace, Erika, Stephanie, and Justin, for never complaining about the countless hours I spent at home studying and preparing to teach other people's children. I want to thank the rest of my family (parents, brothers, grandparents, aunts, uncles, and cousins) for believing in me. Lastly, I want to thank each and every one of my students, because everything I have learned about teaching, I've learned from them.

— Pam —

I am who I am because of the dedication and determination of my ancestors who sacrificed so much that I could be here today. My grandparents, parents, aunts, uncles, and cousins encouraged me to always do my best, and represent our family well. It is their love and support that allowed me to be one of the beneficiaries of the historic legacy of African Americans who struggled for centuries for equality and social justice.

—Kyndall —

We are honored that Dr. Gloria Ladson-Billings wrote the foreword to our book. Our intent is that our book will complement her groundbreaking work on culturally relevant teaching.

We want to thank Dave and Shelley Burgess and the rest of the DBC family for helping us bring this book to fruition.

ABOUT THE AUTHORS

KYNDALL BROWN has over thirty-five years of experience in mathematics education. He was a secondary mathematics teacher in the Los Angeles Unified School District (LAUSD) for thirteen years, teaching at both the middle and high school levels. He has been a professional development provider for over twenty-five years, serving as a mathematics resource teacher for the Los Angeles Systemic Initiative in LAUSD, and as mathematics teacher consultant for and director of the UCLA Mathematics Project (UCLAMP). He is currently the executive director of the California Mathematics Project, a statewide network of professional development organizations.

Kyndall holds a bachelor's degree in mathematics from UC Irvine, master's degrees in computer-based education and mathematics education from CSU Dominguez Hills, and a PhD from UCLA's Graduate School of Education and Information Studies. He also has a single subject credential to teach mathematics in the state of California.

Kyndall has been actively involved in many professional organizations throughout his career, including the Greater Los Angeles Mathematics Council, the California Mathematics Council, the California Association of Mathematics Teacher Educators, the National Council of Teachers of Mathematics, TODOS: Mathematics for ALL, and the Benjamin Banneker Association. Kyndall served a three-year term on the NCTM Professional Development Services Committee and served as the conference chair for the NCTM regional conference in Hartford, Connecticut, October 4–6, 2018. Kyndall served a three-year term on the board of directors of TODOS and served on the committee for the biennial TODOS conference.

Kyndall regularly presents at local, state, and national conferences on various topics related to mathematics education. He writes articles for mathematics education publications. His research interest is the impact of culture and identity on the ways that African American adolescents learn mathematics.

PAMELA SEDA, PhD, is a wife, mother of four adult children, and a math educator with over thirty years of experience. She received a bachelor's degree in mathematics education from the University of South Florida. She completed both her master's degree and PhD in mathematics education at Georgia State University. After working in higher education, Dr. Seda returned to K–12 education as a mathematics teacher, instructional coach, and mathematics coordinator for various school districts in the metro Atlanta area, including Griffin-Spalding County Schools, where she currently serves as the mathematics curriculum coordinator. Dr. Seda presents at numerous state, regional, and national conferences. She is a member of several professional organizations, including TODOS: Mathematics for ALL, Georgia Council of Teachers of Mathematics, and the National Council of Teachers of Mathematics.

She has also served on the board of the Benjamin Banneker Association, the National Council of Supervisors of Mathematics, and Georgia Council of Supervisors of Mathematics. Dr. Seda is the owner of Seda Educational Consulting, LLC, and creator of the VANG math card game. She is passionate about providing positive mathematical experiences for students who have not previously experienced mathematical success. For her, "success" is not simply passing a class, but rather being able to use mathematics as a tool to reason, analyze, communicate, and open doors of opportunity. For this reason, Dr. Seda continually seeks to help all students experience mathematics the way she did—as something positive and empowering.

SPEAKING

Pam and Kyndall regularly present at local, state, and national conferences and provide professional development for schools and districts.

Types of presentations
- Conference workshops
- Professional learning communities
- Consulting with districts
- Coaching support
- School improvement

Topics

- Equity
- Culturally relevant and responsive pedagogy
- Engaging mathematics curriculum/tasks
- Making math accessible

MORE FROM

DAVE BURGESS Consulting, Inc.

Since 2012, DBCI has published books that inspire and equip educators to be their best. For more information on our titles or to purchase bulk orders for your school, district, or book study, visit **DaveBurgessConsulting.com/DBCIbooks**.

MORE FROM THE *LIKE A PIRATE*™ SERIES

Teach Like a PIRATE by Dave Burgess
eXPlore Like a PIRATE by Michael Matera
Learn Like a PIRATE by Paul Solarz
Play Like a PIRATE by Quinn Rollins
Run Like a PIRATE by Adam Welcome
Tech Like a PIRATE by Matt Miller

LEAD LIKE A PIRATE™ SERIES

Lead Like a PIRATE by Shelley Burgess and Beth Houf
Balance Like a PIRATE by Jessica Cabeen, Jessica Johnson, and Sarah Johnson
Lead beyond Your Title by Nili Bartley
Lead with Appreciation by Amber Teamann and Melinda Miller
Lead with Culture by Jay Billy
Lead with Instructional Rounds by Vicki Wilson
Lead with Literacy by Mandy Ellis

LEADERSHIP & SCHOOL CULTURE

Culturize by Jimmy Casas
Escaping the School Leader's Dunk Tank by Rebecca Coda and Rick Jetter
Fight Song by Kim Bearden

From Teacher to Leader by Starr Sackstein

If the Dance Floor Is Empty, Change the Song by Joe Clark

The Innovator's Mindset by George Couros

It's OK to Say "They" by Christy Whittlesey

Kids Deserve It! by Todd Nesloney and Adam Welcome

Let Them Speak by Rebecca Coda and Rick Jetter

The Limitless School by Abe Hege and Adam Dovico

Live Your Excellence by Jimmy Casas

Next-Level Teaching by Jonathan Alsheimer

The Pepper Effect by Sean Gaillard

Principaled by Kate Barker, Kourtney Ferrua, and Rachael George

The Principled Principal by Jeffrey Zoul and Anthony McConnell

Relentless by Hamish Brewer

The Secret Solution by Todd Whitaker, Sam Miller, and Ryan Donlan

Start. Right. Now. by Todd Whitaker, Jeffrey Zoul, and Jimmy Casas

Stop. Right. Now. by Jimmy Casas and Jeffrey Zoul

Teachers Deserve It by Rae Hughart and Adam Welcome

Teach Your Class Off by CJ Reynolds

They Call Me "Mr. De" by Frank DeAngelis

Thrive through the Five by Jill M. Siler

Unmapped Potential by Julie Hasson and Missy Lennard

When Kids Lead by Todd Nesloney and Adam Dovico

Word Shift by Joy Kirr

Your School Rocks by Ryan McLane and Eric Lowe

TECHNOLOGY & TOOLS

50 Things You Can Do with Google Classroom by Alice Keeler and Libbi Miller

50 Things to Go Further with Google Classroom by Alice Keeler and Libbi Miller

140 Twitter Tips for Educators by Brad Currie, Billy Krakower, and Scott Rocco

Block Breaker by Brian Aspinall

Building Blocks for Tiny Techies by Jamila "Mia" Leonard

Code Breaker by Brian Aspinall

The Complete EdTech Coach by Katherine Goyette and Adam Juarez

Control Alt Achieve by Eric Curts

The Esports Education Playbook by Chris Aviles, Steve Isaacs, Christine Lion-Bailey, and Jesse Lubinsky

Google Apps for Littles by Christine Pinto and Alice Keeler

Master the Media by Julie Smith

Reality Bytes by Christine Lion-Bailey, Jesse Lubinsky, and Micah Shippee, PhD

Sail the 7 Cs with Microsoft Education by Becky Keene and Kathi Kersznowski

Shake Up Learning by Kasey Bell

Social LEADia by Jennifer Casa-Todd

Stepping Up to Google Classroom by Alice Keeler and Kimberly Mattina

Teaching Math with Google Apps by Alice Keeler and Diana Herrington

Teachingland by Amanda Fox and Mary Ellen Weeks

TEACHING METHODS & MATERIALS

All 4s and 5s by Andrew Sharos

Boredom Busters by Katie Powell

The Classroom Chef by John Stevens and Matt Vaudrey

The Collaborative Classroom by Trevor Muir

Copyrighteous by Diana Gill

CREATE by Bethany J. Petty

Ditch That Homework by Matt Miller and Alice Keeler

Ditch That Textbook by Matt Miller

Don't Ditch That Tech by Matt Miller, Nate Ridgway, and Angelia Ridgway

EDrenaline Rush by John Meehan

Educated by Design by Michael Cohen, The Tech Rabbi

The EduProtocol Field Guide by Marlena Hebern and Jon Corippo

The EduProtocol Field Guide: Book 2 by Marlena Hebern and Jon Corippo

The EduProtocol Field Guide: Math Edition by Lisa Nowakowski and Jeremiah Ruesch

Game On? Brain On! by Lindsay Portnoy, PhD

Innovating Play by Jessica LaBar-Twomy and Christine Pinto

Instant Relevance by Denis Sheeran

LAUNCH by John Spencer and A. J. Juliani

Make Learning MAGICAL by Tisha Richmond

Pass the Baton by Kathryn Finch and Theresa Hoover

Project-Based Learning Anywhere by Lori Elliott

Pure Genius by Don Wettrick

The Revolution by Darren Ellwein and Derek McCoy

Shift This! by Joy Kirr

Skyrocket Your Teacher Coaching by Michael Cary Sonbert

Spark Learning by Ramsey Musallam

Sparks in the Dark by Travis Crowder and Todd Nesloney

Table Talk Math by John Stevens

Unpack Your Impact by Naomi O'Brien and LaNesha Tabb

The Wild Card by Hope and Wade King

The Writing on the Classroom Wall by Steve Wyborney

INSPIRATION, PROFESSIONAL GROWTH & PERSONAL DEVELOPMENT

Be REAL by Tara Martin

Be the One for Kids by Ryan Sheehy

The Coach ADVenture by Amy Illingworth

Creatively Productive by Lisa Johnson

Educational Eye Exam by Alicia Ray

The EduNinja Mindset by Jennifer Burdis

Empower Our Girls by Lynmara Colón and Adam Welcome

Finding Lifelines by Andrew Grieve and Andrew Sharos

The Four O'Clock Faculty by Rich Czyz

How Much Water Do We Have? by Pete and Kris Nunweiler

P Is for Pirate by Dave and Shelley Burgess

A Passion for Kindness by Tamara Letter

The Path to Serendipity by Allyson Apsey

Sanctuaries by Dan Tricarico

Saving Sycamore by Molly B. Hudgens

The SECRET SAUCE by Rich Czyz

Shattering the Perfect Teacher Myth by Aaron Hogan

Stories from Webb by Todd Nesloney

Talk to Me by Kim Bearden

Teach Better by Chad Ostrowski, Tiffany Ott, Rae Hughart, and Jeff Gargas

Teach Me, Teacher by Jacob Chastain

Teach, Play, Learn! by Adam Peterson

The Teachers of Oz by Herbie Raad and Nathan Lang-Raad

TeamMakers by Laura Robb and Evan Robb

Through the Lens of Serendipity by Allyson Apsey

The Zen Teacher by Dan Tricarico

CHILDREN'S BOOKS

Beyond Us by Aaron Polansky

Cannonball In by Tara Martin

Dolphins in Trees by Aaron Polansky

I Want to Be a Lot by Ashley Savage

The Princes of Serendip by Allyson Apsey

Ride with Emilio by Richard Nares

The Wild Card Kids by Hope and Wade King

Zom-Be a Design Thinker by Amanda Fox

CPSIA information can be obtained
at www.ICGtesting.com
Printed in the USA
FSHW010156151121
85860FS